Lecture Notes in Computer Science 11135

Commenced Publication in 1973
Founding and Former Series Editors:
Gerhard Goos, Juris Hartmanis, and Jan van Leeuwen

More information about this series at http://www.springer.com/series/7408

Raghunath Nambiar · Meikel Poess (Eds.)

Performance Evaluation and Benchmarking for the Era of Artificial Intelligence

10th TPC Technology Conference, TPCTC 2018
Rio de Janeiro, Brazil, August 27–31, 2018
Revised Selected Papers

 Springer

Editors
Raghunath Nambiar
Advanced Micro Systems, Inc.
Santa Clara, CA, USA

Meikel Poess
Oracle Corporation
Redwood Shores, CA, USA

ISSN 0302-9743   ISSN 1611-3349   (electronic)
Lecture Notes in Computer Science
ISBN 978-3-030-11403-9   ISBN 978-3-030-11404-6   (eBook)
https://doi.org/10.1007/978-3-030-11404-6

Library of Congress Control Number: 2018967046

LNCS Sublibrary: SL2 – Programming and Software Engineering

This Springer imprint is published by the registered company Springer Nature Switzerland AG
The registered company address is: Gewerbestrasse 11, 6330 Cham, Switzerland

Preface

The Transaction Processing Performance Council (TPC) is a non-profit organization established in August 1988. Over the years, the TPC has had a significant impact on the computing industry's use of industry-standard benchmarks. Vendors use TPC benchmarks to illustrate performance competitiveness for their existing products, and to improve and monitor the performance of their products under development. Many buyers use TPC benchmark results as points of comparison when purchasing new computing systems.

The information technology landscape is evolving at a rapid pace, challenging industry experts and researchers to develop innovative techniques for evaluation, measurement and characterization of complex systems. The TPC remains committed to developing new benchmark standards to keep pace with these rapid changes in technology. One vehicle for achieving this objective is the TPC's sponsorship of the Technology Conference Series on Performance Evaluation and Benchmarking (TPCTC) established in 2009. With this conference series, the TPC encourages researchers and industry experts to present and debate novel ideas and methodologies in performance evaluation, measurement, and characterization.

The First TPC Technology Conference on Performance Evaluation and Benchmarking (TPCTC 2009) was held in conjunction with the 35th International Conference on Very Large Data Bases (VLDB 2009) in Lyon, France, during August 24–28, 2009.

The Second TPC Technology Conference on Performance Evaluation and Benchmarking (TPCTC 2010) was held in conjunction with the 36th International Conference on Very Large Data Bases (VLDB 2010) in Singapore during September 13–17, 2010.

The Third TPC Technology Conference on Performance Evaluation and Benchmarking (TPCTC 2011) was held in conjunction with the 37th International Conference on Very Large Data Bases (VLDB 2011) in Seattle, Washington, USA, during August 29 – September 3, 2011.

The 4th TPC Technology Conference on Performance Evaluation and Benchmarking (TPCTC 2012) was held in conjunction with the 38th International Conference on Very Large Data Bases (VLDB 2012) in Istanbul, Turkey, during August 27–31, 2012.

The 5th TPC Technology Conference on Performance Evaluation and Benchmarking (TPCTC 2013) was held in conjunction with the 39th International Conference on Very Large Data Bases (VLDB 2013) in Riva del Garda, Italy, during August 26–30, 2013.

The 6th TPC Technology Conference on Performance Evaluation and Benchmarking (TPCTC 2014) was held in conjunction with the 40th International Conference on Very Large Data Bases (VLDB 2014) in Hangzhou, China, during September 1–5, 2014.

The 7th TPC Technology Conference on Performance Evaluation and Benchmarking (TPCTC 2015) was held in conjunction with the 41st International Conference on Very Large Data Bases (VLDB 2015) in Kohala Coast, USA, during August 31 – September 4, 2015.

The 8th TPC Technology Conference on Performance Evaluation and Benchmarking (TPCTC 2016) was held in conjunction with the 42nd International Conference on Very Large Data Bases (VLDB 2016) in New Delhi, India, during September 5–9, 2016.

The 9th TPC Technology Conference on Performance Evaluation and Benchmarking (TPCTC 2017) was held in conjunction with the 43rd International Conference on Very Large Data Bases (VLDB 2017) in Munich, Germany, during August 28 – September 1, 2017.

This book contains the proceedings of the 10th TPC Technology Conference on Performance Evaluation and Benchmarking (TPCTC 2018), held in conjunction with the 44th International Conference on Very Large Data Bases (VLDB 2018) in Rio de Janeiro, Brazil, from August 27th to August 31st, 2018.

The hard work and close cooperation of a number of people have contributed to the success of this conference. We would like to thank the members of TPC and the organizers of VLDB 2018 for their sponsorship; the members of the Program Committee and Publicity Committee for their support; and the authors and the participants who are the primary reason for the success of this conference.

December 2018
Raghunath Nambiar
Meikel Poess

TPCTC 2018 Organization

General Chairs

Raghunath Nambiar, Cisco, USA
Meikel Poess, Oracle, USA

Program Committee

Daniel Bowers, Gartner, USA
Michael Brey, Oracle, USA
Paul Cao, HPE, USA
Alain Crolotte, Teradata Corporation, USA
Ajay Dholakia, Lenovo, USA
Karthik Kulkarni, Cisco, USA
Dhabaleswar Panda, The Ohio State University, USA
Tilmann Rabl, TU Berlin, Germany
Reza Taheri, VMware, USA

Publicity Committee

Raghunath Nambiar, Cisco, USA
Andrew Bond, Red Hat, USA
Paul Cao, HPE, USA
Vo Ngoc Phu, Duy Tan University, Vietnam
Meikel Poess, Oracle, USA
Reza Taheri, VMware, USA
Michael Majdalany, L&M Management Group, USA
Forrest Carman, Owen Media, USA
Andreas Hotea, Hotea Solutions, USA

About the TPC

Introduction to the TPC

The Transaction Processing Performance Council (TPC) is a non-profit organization focused on developing industry standards for data-centric workloads and disseminating vendor-neutral performance data to industry. Additional information is available at http://www.tpc.org/.

TPC Memberships

Full Members

Full Members of the TPC participate in all aspects of the TPC's work, including development of benchmark standards and setting strategic direction. The Full Member application can be found at http://www.tpc.org/information/about/app-member.asp.

Associate Members

Certain organizations may join the TPC as Associate Members. Associate Members may attend TPC meetings, but are not eligible to vote or hold office. Associate membership is available to non-profit organizations, educational institutions, market researchers, publishers, consultants, governments, and businesses that do not create, market, or sell computer products or services. The Associate Member application can be found at http://www.tpc.org/information/about/app-assoc.asp.

Academic and Government Institutions

Academic and government institutions are invited to join the TPC and a special invitation can be found at http://www.tpc.org/information/specialinvitation.asp.

Contact the TPC

TPC
Presidio of San Francisco
Building 572B (surface)
P.O. Box 29920 (mail)
San Francisco, CA 94129-0920
Voice: (+1)415-561-6272
Fax: (+1)415-561-6120
E-mail: info@tpc.org

How to Order TPC Materials

All of our materials are now posted free of charge on our website. If you have any questions, please feel free to contact our office directly or by e-mail at info@tpc.org.

Benchmark Status Report

The TPC Benchmark Status Report is a digest of the activities of the TPC and its technical subcommittees. Sign-up information can be found at the following URL: http://www.tpc.org/information/about/email.asp.

TPC 2018 Organization

Full Members

Actian
Alibaba
AMD
Cisco
Dell EMC
DataCore
Fujitsu
Hewlett Packard Enterprise
Hitachi
Huawei
IBM
Inspur
Intel
Lenovo
Microsoft
Nutanix
Oracle
Pivotal
Red Hat
SAP
Teradata
Transwarp
TTA
VMware

Associate Members

IDEAS International
University of Coimbra, Portugal
China Academy of Information and Communications Technology

Steering Committee

Andrew Bond, Red Hat, USA
Michael Brey (Chair), Oracle, USA
Matthew Emmerton, IBM, USA
Raghunath Nambiar, AMD, USA
Jamie Reding, Microsoft, USA

Public Relations Committee

Andrew Bond, Red Hat, USA
Paul Cao, HPE, USA
Gary Little (Chair), Nutanix
Raghunath Nambiar, AMD, USA
Meikel Poess, Oracle, USA
Reza Taheri, VMware, USA

Technical Advisory Board

Paul Cao, HPE, USA
Matthew Emmerton, IBM, USA
Gary Little, Nutanix
Jamie Reding (Chair), Microsoft, USA
Da-Qi Ren, Huawei, USA
Ken Rule, Intel, USA
Nicholas Wakou, Dell, USA

Technical Subcommittees and Chairs

TPC-C: Jamie Reding, Microsoft, USA
TPC-H: Meikel Poess, Oracle, USA
TPC-E: Matthew Emmerton, IBM, USA
TPC-DS: Meikel Poess, Oracle, USA
TPC-DI: Meikel Poess, Oracle, USA
TPCx-HS: Tariq Magdon-Ismail, VMware, USA
TPCx-BB: Bhaskar Gowda, Intel, USA
TPCx-V: Reza Taheri, VMware, USA
TPCx-HCI: Reza Taheri, VMware, USA
TPCx-IoT: Karthik Kulkarni, Cisco, USA
TPC-Pricing: Jamie Reding, Microsoft, USA
TPC-Energy: Paul Cao, HPE, USA

Working Group and Chair

TPC-AI: Raghunath Nambiar, AMD, USA

Contents

Industry Panel on Defining Industry Standards for Benchmarking Artificial Intelligence

Raghunath Nambiar[1(✉)], Shahram Ghandeharizadeh[2], Gary Little[3], Christoph Boden[4], and Ajay Dholakia[5]

[1] AMD, Inc., Santa Clara, USA
raghu.nambiar@amd.com
[2] University of Southern California, Los Angeles, USA
shahram@usc.edu
[3] Nutanix, Inc., San Jose, USA
gary@nutanix.com
[4] Technischen Universität Berlin, Berlin, Germany
christoph.boden@tu-berlin.de
[5] Lenovo Group Limited, Morrisville, USA
adholakia@lenovo.com

Abstract. Introduced in 2009, the Technology Conference on Performance Evaluation and Benchmarking (TPCTC) is a forum bringing together industry experts and researchers to develop innovative techniques for evaluation, measurement and characterization. This panel at the tenth TPC Technology Conference on Performance Evaluation and Benchmarking (TPCTC 2018) brought together industry experts and researchers from a broad spectrum of interests in the field of Artificial Intelligence (AI).

1 Transaction Processing Performance Council: A Look Back

The Transaction Processing Performance Council (TPC) was created to develop standards and benchmarks that can be used by vendors, customers and researchers to characterize system performance and total cost of ownership for different types of workloads. At first, the TPC focused on defining benchmark standards for transaction processing. Later, in line with industry trends, the TPC expanded its focus to decision support systems, data integration, virtualization, big data analytics, internet of things and hyperconverged infrastructure. These benchmarks create a level playing field and are used to drive innovation, enabling an iterative process whose end result is higher performing, lower cost systems with more efficient energy usage [1–4].

Today, the TPC defines two benchmark classes: Enterprise and Express. See Fig. 1 [2].

- Enterprise benchmarks are technology agnostic. They are specification-based, typically complex, and have long development cycles. Their specifications are provided by the TPC, but their implementation is up to the vendor. The vendor may

© Springer Nature Switzerland AG 2019
R. Nambiar and M. Poess (Eds.): TPCTC 2018, LNCS 11135, pp. 1–6, 2019.
https://doi.org/10.1007/978-3-030-11404-6_1

choose any commercially available combination of software and hardware products to implement the benchmark.

Enterprise benchmarks are:
  TPC-C: transaction processing
  TPC-E: transaction processing
  TPC-H: decision support systems
  TPC-DS: complex decision support systems and big data analytics
  TPC-DI: data integration
  TPC-VMS: database virtualization

- Express benchmarks are kit-based, typically using existing workloads, and have shorter development cycles. Using the TPC-provided kits is required for the publication of express benchmarks.

Express benchmarks are:
  TPCx-HS: big data systems (based on Hadoop)
  TPCx-HS V2: big data systems (based on Hadoop and Spark)
  TPCx-BB: big data systems (based on Hadoop)
  TPCx-V: database virtualization
  TPCx-IoT: internet of things
  TPCx-HCI: hyperconverged infrastructure.

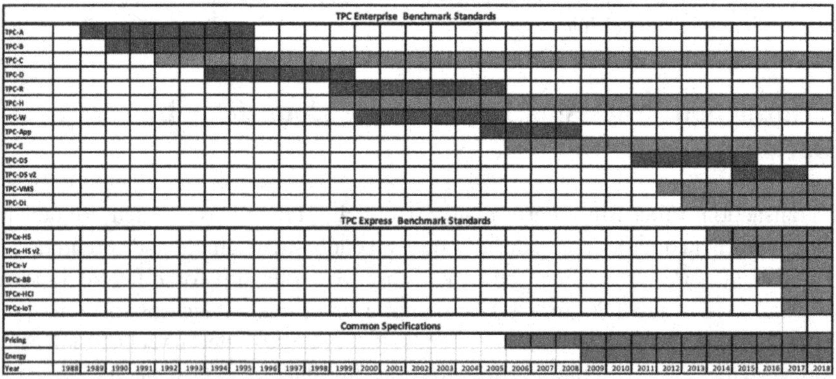

Fig. 1. TPC benchmark standards

Additionally, the TPC has introduced two specifications: pricing specification (TPC-Pricing), and energy specification (TPC-Energy). These are common across all current standards.

2   Formation of TPC Artificial Intelligence Working Group

The TPC has a long history of keeping pace with innovations in technology. Artificial Intelligence has unique qualities that introduce new challenges, and it is for this reason the TPC has formed a working group (TPC-AI) tasked with developing industry standard benchmarks for both hardware and software platforms associated with running Artificial Intelligence based workloads [5]. The working group will define the key characteristics of these systems, identify the areas with the greatest potential for improvement through performance optimization, and work to understand the key factors for customers when making purchasing decisions.

3   Panel Discussion

The panel talked about the market segment, use cases and some of the key considerations.

Artificial Intelligence Today: Years of research into creating AI are finally starting to yield practical real-world applications. The combination of increased computational power, research enabling the creation of deep neural networks, the harnessing of big data, and improvements in the methods to train machine learning systems has created the opportunity for completely new, often disruptive technologies that provide concrete value and a competitive edge to today's organizations.

Everyday interactions with Artificial Intelligence are now commonplace in applications ranging from speech recognition and natural language processing to sentiment analysis and recommendation engines. Applications utilizing computer vision are now being deployed, from the relatively simple license plate reader to the very complex facial recognition systems. More ambitious projects, like autonomous vehicles, are being actively pursued.

Artificial Intelligence and machine learning systems operate in a fundamentally different manner than traditional data processing systems. Unlike traditional systems, Machine Learning systems are not programmed with specific logic. Instead, they are supplied with huge datasets and employ algorithms that identify the patterns and relationships in the data. This, in turn, requires new ways to evaluate the efficacy of the various hardware and software solutions used to implement Artificial Intelligence and Machine Learning.

Significant investments have been made in Artificial Intelligence. According to McKinsey & Company, tech giants spent $20 billion to $30 billion in 2016 on Artificial Intelligence, 90% of this was spent on research and developments and 10% on acquisitions.

AI Use Cases: AI is currently seeing everyday use in applications as diverse as speech recognition, sentiment analysis and natural language processing (including language translation), computer vision and image recognition, autonomous vehicles and recommendation engines. It is a rapidly-growing area, being evaluated for a broad array of use cases across consumer, enterprise, and government markets [4, 6]. See Fig. 2.

Fig. 2. AI opportunities across industries

Benchmark Considerations: There are five key aspects that all good benchmarks have, and benchmarks for Artificial Intelligence are no exception. See Fig. 3 [7]:

- Relevant - to the user of the benchmark (engineering, marketing, buyers, researchers)
- Repeatable – repeatable in terms of completion time and same results
- Fairness – to the various hardware and software technologies that are part of the system
- Verifiability – confidence that the test results are real with some sort of audit process
- Economical – economical to set up, run and publish the results.

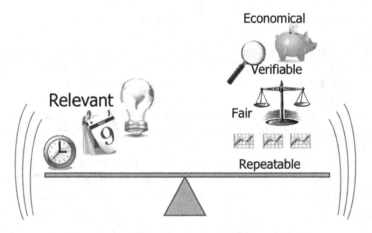

Fig. 3. Five characteristics of a good benchmark [7]

4   About the Panelists

- Ajay Dholakia is a Principal Engineer, Senior Solution Architect and Chief Technologist for Software, Solutions and Networking Development within Lenovo Data Center Group. In this role, he is leading the development of customer solutions in the areas of AI, big data, analytics and cloud computing. He is also driving new projects for solution development using emerging technologies including Internet of Things (IoT) and blockchain. In his career spanning over 25 years, he has led diverse projects in research, technology, product and solution development and business/technical strategy. Prior to joining Lenovo, he spent 19 years at IBM working on data communication, data storage and compute server technologies. Ajay holds more than 50 patents and has authored over 40 technical publications including the book "Introduction to Convolutional Codes with Applications." Ajay earned a B. E. (Hons.) in Electrical and Electronics Engineering from the Birla Institute of Technology and Science in India, an MBA from the Henley Business School in the U.K. and M.S. and Ph.D. in Electrical and Computer Engineering from North Carolina State University, Raleigh, NC, USA.
- Christoph Boden is a research associate at the Database Systems and Information Management group at TU Berlin and at the German Research Center for Artificial Intelligence (DFKI). He is part of the management of the Berlin Big Data Center (BBDC) research project. In his research he focuses on benchmarking data processing systems for scalable machine learning workloads.
- Gary Little is a performance engineer at Nutanix focusing on the intersection of high performance and highly resilient systems. His early career was with Sun Solaris systems running Oracle databases. In 2015, his work on performance and resilience came to fruition as the Nutanix X-Ray product. X-Ray allows end-users to formulate and execute complex, resilience centered testing. He brought similar ideas into the TPC that subsequently became part of the TPCx-HCI benchmark.
- Shahram Ghandeharizadeh directs the database laboratory at the USC Computer Science department. His research team has been investigating design and implementation of scalable, highly available, and elastic data infrastructure for more than two decades. He is the co-inventor of BG, a benchmark for interactive social networking actions. His research has been recognized with numerous awards including the prestigious ACM Software System Award.
- Raghunath Nambiar is the Corporate Vice President and Chief Technology Officer of Datacenter Ecosystems and Application Engineering at AMD. He brings years of technical accomplishments with significant expertise in systems architecture, performance engineering, and creating disruptive technology solutions. Raghu has served in leadership positions on industry standards committees for performance evaluation and leading academic conferences. He is the chairman of the TPC's benchmark standards committee for Artificial Intelligence. He chaired the industry's first standards committee for benchmarking big data systems, the industry's first standards committee for benchmarking Internet of Things, and is the founding chair of TPC's International Conference Series on Performance Evaluation and Benchmarking. Raghu has published more than 50 peer-reviewed papers and holds eight

patents with several pending. He is the author of "Transforming Industry Through Data Analytics: Digital Disruption in Cities, Energy, Manufacturing, Healthcare, and Transportation".

Acknowledgements. The panelists acknowledge the contributions of the TPC members to the industry and academic community and look forward to working with the TPC AI committee in creating a new standard for benchmarking AI systems. The panelists also thank Shane Handy for his comments and feedback with this document.

References

1. Stonebraker, M.: A new direction for TPC? In: Nambiar, R., Poess, M. (eds.) TPCTC 2009. LNCS, vol. 5895, pp. 11–17. Springer, Heidelberg (2009). https://doi.org/10.1007/978-3-642-10424-4_2
2. Nambiar, R., Poess, M.: Keeping the TPC relevant! PVLDB **6**(11), 1186–1187 (2013)
3. Nambiar, R., Wakou, N., Carman, F., Majdalany, M.: Transaction Processing Performance Council (TPC): state of the council 2010. In: Nambiar, R., Poess, M. (eds.) TPCTC 2010. LNCS, vol. 6417, pp. 1–9. Springer, Heidelberg (2011). https://doi.org/10.1007/978-3-642-18206-8_1
4. Nambiar, R.: Towards an industry standard for benchmarking artificial intelligence systems. In: ICDE 2018, pp. 1679–1680 (2018)
5. TPC Press Release Transaction Processing Performance Council (TPC) Establishes Artificial Intelligence Working Group (TPC-AI). https://www.businesswire.com/news/home/20171212005281/en/Transaction-Processing-Performance-Council-TPC-Establishes-Artificial
6. Cisco Blog: Towards an Industry Standard for Benchmarking AI. https://blogs.cisco.com/datacenter/towards-an-industry-standard-for-benchmarking-ai
7. Huppler, K.: The art of building a good benchmark. In: Nambiar, R., Poess, M. (eds.) TPCTC 2009. LNCS, vol. 5895, pp. 18–30. Springer, Heidelberg (2009). https://doi.org/10.1007/978-3-642-10424-4_3
8. McKinsey Global Institute: Artificial Intelligence the Next Digital Fortier? Decision Paper, June 2017

UniBench: A Benchmark for Multi-model Database Management Systems

Chao Zhang, Jiaheng Lu$^{(\boxtimes)}$, Pengfei Xu, and Yuxing Chen

Department of Computer Science, University of Helsinki, Helsinki, Finland
Jiaheng.Lu@helsinki.fi

Abstract. Unlike traditional database management systems which are organized around a single data model, a multi-model database (MMDB) utilizes a single, integrated back-end to support multiple data models, such as document, graph, relational, and key-value. As more and more platforms are proposed to deal with multi-model data, it becomes crucial to establish a benchmark for evaluating the performance and usability of MMDBs. Previous benchmarks, however, are inadequate for such scenario because they lack a comprehensive consideration for multiple models of data. In this paper, we present a benchmark, called UniBench, with the goal of facilitating a holistic and rigorous evaluation of MMDBs. UniBench consists of a mixed data model, a synthetic multi-model data generator, and a set of core workloads. Specifically, the data model simulates an emerging application: Social Commerce, a Web-based application combining E-commerce and social media. The data generator provides diverse data format including JSON, XML, key-value, tabular, and graph. The workloads are comprised of a set of multi-model queries and transactions, aiming to cover essential aspects of multi-model data management. We implemented all workloads on ArangoDB and OrientDB to illustrate the feasibility of our proposed benchmarking system and show the learned lessons through the evaluation of these two multi-model databases. The source code and data of this benchmark can be downloaded at http://udbms.cs.helsinki.fi/bench/.

1 Introduction

Multi-Model DataBase (MMDB) is an emerging trend for the database management system [16,17], which utilizes a single platform to manage data stored in different models, such as document, graph, relational, and key-value. Compared to the polyglot persistence technology [24] that employs separate data stores to satisfy various use cases, MMDB is considered as the next generation of data management system incorporating flexibility, scalability, and consistency. The recent Gartner Magic quadrant [9] for operational database management systems predicts that, in the near future, all leading operational DBMSs will offer multiple data models in a unified platform. MMDB is beneficial for modern applications that require dealing with heterogeneous data sources while embracing the

© Springer Nature Switzerland AG 2019
R. Nambiar and M. Poess (Eds.): TPCTC 2018, LNCS 11135, pp. 7–23, 2019.
https://doi.org/10.1007/978-3-030-11404-6_2

agile development. For instance, in a *Social Commerce* application [27], enterprises often gain business insights by integrating graphs from social networks, documents from the purchase history, and tables from customer information. Data scientists usually write scripts for each data model separately, then wrangles them into a unified form to proceed with real-time and OLAP analysis. However, as the scale and complexity of data increase, such method becomes tedious and inefficient. By leveraging the power of MMDB, one can easily ingest and analyze heterogeneous data in real time and hence swiftly adjust the operational strategy.

Database benchmark becomes an essential tool for the evaluation and comparison of DBMSs since the advent of Wisconsin benchmark [5] in the early 1980s. Since then, many database benchmarks have been proposed by academia and industry for various evaluation goals, such as TPC-C [25] for RDBMSs, TPC-DI [21] for data integration; OO7 benchmark [2] for object-oriented DBMSs, and XML benchmark systems [15,23] for XML DBMSs. More recently, the NoSQL and big data movement in the late 2000s brought the arrival of the next generation of benchmarks, such as YCSB benchmark [4] for cloud serving systems, LDBC [6] for Graph and RDF DBMSs, BigBench [3,10] for big data systems. However, those general-purpose or micro benchmarks are not designed for MMDBs. As more and more platforms are proposed to deal with multi-model data, it becomes important to have a benchmark for evaluating the performance of MMDBs and comparing different multi-model approaches.

In general, there are two challenges evaluating the performance of MMDBs:

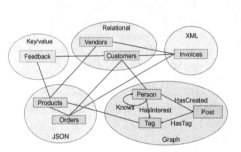

Fig. 1. Unibench data model

The first challenge is to generate synthetic multi-model data. First, existing data generators cannot be directly adopted to evaluate MMDBs because they only involve one model. Besides, combining them reasonably is a difficult task since each generator simulates a particular scenario. In this study, we develop a new data generator to provide correlated data in diverse models. As shown in Fig. 1, our benchmark system consists of five data models, i.e., Graph, Relational, JSON, Key-value, and XML. It simulates a *social commerce* scenario [27] that combines the social network with the E-commerce context. The relational model includes the structured *customers* and *vendors*, JSON model contains the semi-structured *orders* and *products*. The social network is modeled as graph, which includes three entities and four relations. i.e., *person, post, tag, person_knows_person, person_has_tag, person_create_post, post_has_tag. Feedback* and *Invoices* are modeled as key-value and XML, respectively. These also have correlations across the data models. For instance, customer *knows* friends (relational correlates with the graph model), customer *makes* transactions. (JSON correlates with relational model). Furthermore, we propose a three-phase framework to simulate customers' behaviors in social commerce. This framework consists of purchase, propagation-purchase, and re-purchase, which takes into account a variety of factors to generate the Power-law distribution data that are widely seen in real life. Particularly, we propose a new probabilistic model CLVSC (Customer Lifetime Value in Social Commerce) to make fine-grained predictions in the third phase.

The second challenge is to design multi-model workloads. Such workloads are the fundamental operations in many complex and modern applications. However, little attention has been paid to study them. It is non-trivial to design the workloads which not only cover the most important paradigms of multi-model query processing but also simulate realistic use cases. In this regard, we first simulate meaningful business cases in social commerce by dividing them into four layers: *individual, conversation, community,* and *commerce.* Then we define a set of multi-model queries and transactions based on the choke point technique [22], which tests the weak points of databases to make the benchmark challenging and interesting. Choke points of our benchmark workloads involve performances of the multi-model aggregation, join, and transaction, demanding the database to determine the optimal multi-model join order, handle the complex aggregations, and guarantee the concurrency and efficiency simultaneously.

We summarize our contributions as follows:

1. We develop a new data generator, which provides correlated data in diverse data models. We also propose a three-phase framework to generate data for modeling the customers' behaviors in social commerce. We implement the generator on the top of Spark and Hadoop to provide efficiency and scalability.
2. We design a set of multi-model workloads including ten queries and two transactions from technical and business perspectives.
3. We implement proposed workloads and conduct experiments on two MMDBs: ArangoDB [1] and OrientDB [19]. We analytically report the performance comparison and our learned lessons.

The rest of this paper is divided as follows. Section 2 introduces the background and related work. Section 3 illustrates the workflow of data generation. Section 4 presents the multi-model workload in detail. The experimental results are shown in Section 5. Finally, Sect. 6 concludes this work.

2   Background and Related Work

Background. Multi-model data management is proposed to address the "*Variety*" challenge of data in a complex world. The first evolution is the prevalence of *Polyglot Persistence* [24] method, which exploits numerous databases to handle different forms of data and integrates them to provide a unified interface. Unfortunately, such method imposes further operational complexity and cost, because the need for integrating multiple databases has a significant engineering and operational overhead. The drawback of *Polyglot Persistence* leads to the

Table 1. Comparison of multi-model DBMSs

System	Query language	Primary model	Secondary model	Storage strategy
AgensGraph	OpenCypher, SQL	Relational	Graph, JSON	One engine
ArangoDB	AQL	JSON	Graph, Key-value	One engine
OrientDB	SQL-like	Graph	JSON, Key-value	One engine
Marklogic	Xpath	XML	JSON, RDF	One engine
Redis	API	Key-value	Graph, JSON	One engine
NitrosBase	SparQL, SQL	RDF	Graph, JSON, Key-value	One engine
Datastax	CQL	Column	JSON, Graph	Multiple engines
DynamoDB	API, SQL	-	JSON, Graph, Key-value	Multiple engines
CosmosDB	API, SQL	-	**ALL** but XML	Multiple engines
Oracle 12c	SQL-extension	Relational	**ALL**	**Both**

second evolution of multi-model data management. First, many SQL-extension ecosystems and NoSQL systems have been transformed to multi-model systems by integrating additional engines or functions into a unified platform for supporting additional models. On the other hand, there emerge many native multi-model databases, e.g., ArangoDB, AgensGraph, OrientDB. These systems utilize a single store to manage the multi-model data, along with a unified or hybrid query language. Table 1 shows the representatives of MMDBs compared by several properties, namely, query language, primary model, secondary model, and storage strategy. The secondary model of each system is extended in the second evolution. Redis, for example, adds JSON and graph to its key-value store. On the other hand, DynamoDB employs several engines to support multiple models including JSON, graph, and key-value, and it has no specified primary model because each model is regarded as the first-class citizen.

Related Work. There are a few works on multi-model data modeling, data generation and database benchmarking. In [16], we have envisioned a multi-model database benchmark system (but without any detailed solution and implementation). Regarding the data modeling and data generation, TPC-DI [21] features a multi-model input data including XML, CSV, and textual parts, which is used to evaluate the transformation cost in data integration process. Also, Bigbench [10] incorporates semi-structured (logs) and unstructured data (reviews) into TPC-DS's structured data. However, no consideration was given to JSON and graph, which are currently two most popular models in data management. As for the performance evaluation, several evaluation efforts [18,20] have been done on multi-model databases recently. Nevertheless, they only focus on simple workloads, such as CRUD operation, aggregation, graph depth traversal, which are inadequate since they do not account for complex workloads concerning multi-model characteristics.

The most relevant work about our approach is LDBC social network benchmark [6]. First, our graph generation is based on LDBC [6], we choose it as the starting point for its scalability and rich semantics in simulating social networks. It also supports the generation of correlated graph by leveraging the MapReduce paradigm of Hadoop. However, since our goal is concentrating on benchmarking multi-model databases rather than graph databases, we have simplified the graph complexity to better fit our goal. Moreover, in order to generate the E-commerce transactions with associated graph entities, we replace some of its dictionaries by collecting commerce metadata from Amazon review [14] and DBpedia dataset [13]. Second, our workload design is motivated by LDBC [6], TPC-C [25] and Bigbench [10]. In particular, LDBC follows the graph-based choke points approach, and Bigbench focuses on the business questions in five main categories. Motivated by these two design principles, we also propose the choke-point and business-driven query design. For the transaction design, despite the business cases of two proposed transactions e.g., New Order and Payment are similar to those in TPC-C [25], the data involved in our benchmark systems come from multiple data models. Therefore we focus on the multi-model transactions rather than single-model transactions.

3   Data Generation

In this section, we introduce the process of multi-model data generation. Figure 2 shows our three-phase data generation framework. Specifically, (i) in *Purchase* phase, LDBC [6] obtains metadata from the repository, then generates graph data and initial interests of persons. These data is feed to our generator to produce transaction data. (ii) In *Propagation-Purchase* phase, interests of cold-start customers are generated based on information obtained in the previous phase. (iii) In *Re-purchase* phase, interests of all customers will be generated based on CLVSV model, which is discussed shortly. In each phase, we generate transaction data according to the interests of customers and unite all three portions as an integral part of the multi-model dataset. The entire generation process is presented in Algorithm 1, and discussed in detail as follows:

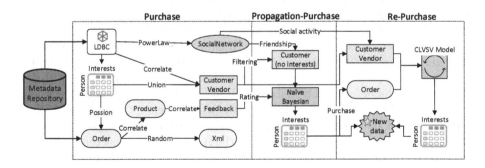

Fig. 2. Data generation workflow.

Algorithm 1. Data Generation

Input: Scale factor f, constant c controlling number of transaction, real value
        λ as Poisson parameter, and meta data
Output: Multi-model dataset D

1 $G \leftarrow LDBC(f)$ // graph data generated by the LDBC generator
2 $R \leftarrow$ relational data transformed from graph and meta data
3 $L_1 \leftarrow$ initial list of purchase interest of persons from G
4 $J, X, KV, D \leftarrow \varnothing$ // initial sets of JSON, XML, Key-value, and output
5 $P_t, P_f \leftarrow$ persons having interests, persons having no interests
6 **foreach** $p \in P_t$ **do**
7       $count \leftarrow L_1/c$
8   **while** $count \neq 0$ **do**
9            $r \leftarrow Poisson(\lambda)$
10           $count \leftarrow count - 1$
11           $J, X, KV \leftarrow Purchase(r, p)$ // generate transaction data
12           $D \leftarrow D \cup J \cup X \cup KV$
13 BayesModel $\leftarrow$ fit the bayes model based on R and KV
14 **foreach** $p \in P_f$ **do**
15      $L_2 \leftarrow$ generate new interest list based on equation 1
16      $D \leftarrow D \cup Propagation\text{-}Purchase(p, L_2)$
17 CLVSC $\leftarrow$ fit the CLVSC model based on a small portion of samples
18 **foreach** $p \in P_t \cup P_f$ **do**
19      $L_3 \leftarrow \overline{CLVSC(J, G)}$ // generate new interests by CLVSC model
20      $D \leftarrow D \cup Re\text{-}Purchase(p, L_3)$ // generate new transaction data
21 **return** D

3.1 Purchase

In this phase, we consider two factors when generating the data. First, persons usually buy products based on their interests. Second, persons with more interests are more likely to buy products than others. The person's interests for the products are generated by the LDBC. This phase is implemented on the top of Spark SQL using Scala, which utilizes a plentiful APIs and UDFs to generate the multi-model data. Specifically, we first determine the number of transactions for each person by dividing the number of their interests with a constant c, then select the size for each transaction from a Poisson distribution with parameter λ, finally assign items to each transaction by randomly choosing items from their interest sets. The *orders* will be output in JSON format with an embedded item array of orderline. Meanwhile, The *invoices* will be generated with the same information but in XML format. In addition, we randomly select the product's real review and corresponding rating from the Amazon dataset as the feedback. Consequently, our data consist of five models: *social network* (Graph), *vendor* and *customer* (Relation), *order and product* (JSON), *invoice* (XML), *feedback* (Key-value).

3.2   Propagation-Purchase

In this phase, we incorporate two ingredients from previous data generation: (i) person's basic demographic data, e.g., gender, age, location. (ii) feedback of friends. This is motivated by the observation that people with same attributes more likely have the same behaviors, and people also trust the product recommendations from friends. The scoring function is defined as follow:

$$S_{ui} = \sum_k k \times Pr(R_{ui} = k | A = a_u) + E(R_{vi} : \forall v \in N(u)) \tag{1}$$

where $\sum_k k \times Pr(R_{ui} = k | A = a_u)$ is the expectation of the probability distribution of the target user u's rating on the target item i, and $A = \{a_1, a_2, \ldots, a_m\}$ is user attribute set computed based on Naive Bayesian method. The latter part $E(R_{vi} : \forall v \in N(u))$ is the expectation of u's friends' rating distribution on the target item, where $N(u)$ is the friends set of user u, and the item i is from the purchase transaction of friends. To train the bayes model, we implemented our techniques using Python's scikit-learn, which takes users' profiles and rating history from the previous phase as the training set. For each person without interests, we take the items rated by their friends as the candidate set, then rank them using Eq. (1). Finally, we take the first n percent portion as the new interests, and then generate the new transactions the same as the process in the purchase phase.

3.3   Re-purchase

The CLV (Customer Lifetime Value) model [11] is proposed to address the RFM's limitation in forecasting non-contractual customer behavior. We propose a new probabilistic model CLVSC (Customer Lifetime Value in Social Commerce) to make fine-grained predictions by incorporating the customer's social activities regarding the brand. In general, the CLVSC is comprised of three components: the expected number of behaviors, the expected monetary value, and the expected positive social engagement of customer. The scoring function for CLVSC is defined as follow:

$$\begin{aligned} S_{ib}(CLVSC) &= E(X^* \,|\, n^*, x', n, m, \alpha, \beta, \gamma, \delta) \\ &\quad \times (E(M \,|\, p, q, \upsilon, m_x, x) + E(S \,|\, \bar{s}, \theta, \tau)) \end{aligned} \tag{2}$$

where i and b are the customer and brand index, respectively,

$E(X^* | n^*, x', n, m, \alpha, \beta, \gamma, \delta)$ denote the expected number of behaviors over the next n^* periods by a customer with observed behavior history (x', n, m), where x' is the number of behavior that occurred in n period, with the last behavior m $\leqslant$ n; (α, β) and (γ, δ) are the beta distribution parameters for active probability and inactive probability respectively, the behavior is either the purchase or the post. Utilizing the beta-geometric/beta-binomial (BG/BB) [7] model, we have

$$E(X^* \mid n^*, x', n, m, \alpha, \beta, \gamma, \delta)$$
$$= \frac{B(\alpha + x + 1, \beta + n - x)}{B(\alpha, \beta)}$$
$$\times \frac{B(\gamma - 1, \delta + n + 1) - B(\gamma - 1, \delta + n + n^* + 1)}{B(\gamma, \delta)} \tag{3}$$
$$\div L(\alpha, \beta, \gamma, \delta \mid x, n, m)$$

where L($\cdot$) is the likelihood function. This result is derived from taking the expectation over the joint posterior distribution of active probability and inactive probability.

$E(M \mid p, q, v, m_x, x)$ denote the expected monetary value. Following the Fader, Hardie, and Berger's approach [8] of adding monetary value, we have

$$E(M \mid p, q, v, m_x, x)$$
$$= \left(\frac{q - 1}{px + q - 1} \right) \frac{vp}{q - 1} + \left(\frac{px}{px + q - 1} \right) m_x \tag{4}$$

$E(S \mid \bar{s}, \theta, \tau)$ denote the expected social engagement of customer, we assume that the number of social engagement of customer follows a Poisson process with rate λ, and heterogeneity in λ follows a gamma distribution with shape parameter θ and rate parameter τ across customers. According to the conjugation of Poisson-gamma model, the point estimate $E(S \mid \bar{s}, \theta, \tau)$ can be factorized as follow,

$$E(S \mid \bar{s}, \theta, \tau) = \theta' \tau' = \frac{\tau}{1 + \tau} \bar{s} + \frac{\tau}{1 + \tau} \theta \tau \tag{5}$$

The resulting point estimate is therefore a weighted average of the sample mean $\bar{s}$ and the prior mean $\theta \tau$.

We implemented the CLVSC model using R's BTYD package [26], which takes a small portion of samples from the previous phases as the training set. For all persons, we estimate their interests of brands, then acquire the m interests from top n brands, finally generate the new transactions the same as the process in the purchase phase.

4   Workload

The UniBench workload consists of a set of complex read-only queries and read-write transactions that involve at least two data models, aiming to cover different business cases and technical perspectives. More specifically, as for business cases, they fall into four main levers [12]: *individual, conversation, community*, and *commerce*. In these four levers, common-used business cases in different granularity are rendered. Regarding technical perspectives, they are designed based on the *choke-point* technique [22] which combines common technical challenges with new intractable problems for the multi-model query processing, ranging from the conjunctive queries (OLTP) to analysis (OLAP) workloads. Their characteristics are summarized in Table 2. Note that in the description column, the italic and bold texts denote the intended input and output data, respectively.

Table 2. Characteristics of workload

Label	Business category	Technique dimension	Description
Q1	Individual	Perform point query on a customer's all multi-model data	For a given *customer*, find her **profile, orders, feedback**, and **posts**
Q2	Conversation	Join data from Relation, Graph, and JSON	For a given *product*, find the **persons** who had bought it and posted on it
Q3	Conversation	Join data from Relation, Graph, and Key-value, filter structured and unstructured data	For a given *product*, find **persons** who have commented and posted on it, and detect negative **sentiments** from them
Q4	Community	Aggregate and sort the JSON order, Perform the 3-hop graph traversal in the subgraph, return the intersection of two sets	Find the top-2 **persons** who spend the highest amount of money in orders. Then for each person, traverse her knows-graph with 3-hop to find the friends, and finally return the common **friends** of these two persons
Q5	Community	Join data from Relation, Graph, and Key-value with two predicates, recursive path query for Graph, embedded array operation for JSON, and composited-key lookup for Key-value	Given a start *customer* and a product *category*, find **persons** who are this customer's friends within 3-hop friendships in knows-graph, and they have bought products in the given category. Finally, return **feedback** with the 5-rating review of those bought products
Q6	Community	Perform the shortest path calculations between two nodes, find the correlated JSON orders of nodes in the path, aggregation on returned JSON orders	Given *customer 1* and *customer 2*, find persons in the **shortest path** between them in the subgraph, and return the TOP 3 **best sellers** from all these persons' purchases
Q7	Commerce	Join data from Relation, JSON and Key-value, compare the aggregation results between two periods, identify the reviews with negative sentiment	For the *products* of a given *vendor* with declining sales compare to the former quarter, analyze the **reviews** for these items to see if there are any negative sentiments

(*continued*)

Table 2. (*continued*)

Label	Business category	Technique dimension	Description
Q8	Commerce	Perform the embedded array filtering and aggregation on JSON order, aggregate the correlated graph data for each records	For all the *products* of a given *category* during a given year, compute its **total sales amount**, and measure its **popularity** in the social media
Q9	Commerce	Perform the embedded array filtering, aggregation, and sorting on JSON order, then find the correlated graph data	Find top-3 **companies** who have the largest amount of sales at one *country*, for each company, compare the number of the male and female customers, and return the most recent **posts** of them
Q10	Commerce	Perform the aggregation and sort on graph data, then find the correlated Key-value and JSON data	Find the top-10 most active **persons** by aggregating the *posts* during the last year, then calculate their **RFM (Recency, Frequency, Monetary) value** in the same period, and return their recent **reviews** and tags of **interest**
T1	New order transaction	Check the ACID properties and evaluate the efficiency on read-heavy multi-model transaction that involves JSON and XML	(i) Create and insert the **order**, (ii) update the quantity of involved **products**, (iii) insert the **invoice**
T2	Payment transaction	Check the ACID properties and evaluate the efficiency on write-heavy multi-model transaction that involves Relation, JSON and XML	(i) Retrieve the unpaid **order**, (ii) update the balance of the **seller** and **buyer**, (iii) update the **order** status to paid, (iv) update the related **invoice**

4.1 Business Cases

We identify two transactions and four layers of queries that include ten multi-model queries to simulate realistic business cases in social commerce. Specifically, the two transactions, namely, *New Order* and *Payment* transactions, simulates the huge parallel transactions for online shopping. They represent heavy-weight, read-write transactions with a high frequency of execution to satisfy on-line users. As for multi-model queries, the **individual level** mimics the case that companies build a 360-degree customer view by gathering data from customer's multiple sources. There is one query for this level. **conversation level** focus on analyzing the customer's semi-structured and unstructured data, including Query 2 and 3. The two queries are commonly used for the company to capture customer's sentiment polarity from the feedback and then adjust the online advertising or operation strategy. Query 4, 5, 6, in the **community level** target at two areas: mining common purchase patterns in a community and analyzing the community's influence on the individual's purchase behaviors. Finally, **commerce level** aims at the assortment optimization and performance transparency. Specifically, Query 7, 8, 9 identify products or vendors with downward or upward performance and then find the cause for improvements. Query 10 is to compute the Recency, Frequency, Monetary (RFM) value of customers regarding the vendor, and then find the common tags in the posts.

4.2   Technical Dimensions

Our workload design is based on the *choke point* technique that tests many aspects of the database when handling the query. Typically, these aspects may concern different components of databases, such as the query optimizer, the execution engine, and the storage system. Moreover, the choke points in our workload not only involve common query processing challenges for the traditional database systems but also take a few new problems of multi-model query processing. Here we list three key points:

Choosing the Right Join Type and Order. Determining the proper join type and order for multi-model queries is a new and non-trivial problem. This is because it demands the query optimizer to estimate the cardinality with respect to involved models. Moreover, it needs the query optimizer to judiciously determine the optimal join order for multi-model query. The execution time of different join orders and types may vary by orders of magnitude due to the domination of different data model. Therefore, this choke point tests the query optimizer's ability to find an optimal join type and order for the multi-model query. In our proposed workload, all the queries involve multiple joins across different data model.

Performing Complex Aggregation. This choke-point includes two types of queries concerning the complex aggregation. The first type is the aggregation towards the complex data structure which requires MMDB to deal with schema-agnostic data when proceeding with aggregation. The second one is the query with subsequent aggregations, where the results of an aggregation serve as the input of another aggregation. Also, these aggregations involve the union of multiple models' results. For instance, Query 10 requires the MMDB to access the product array in the JSON orders when processing the first aggregation. Then the results will be an input for the second aggregation in the Graph.

Ensuring the Consistency and Efficiency. A database transaction should possess ACID properties. Therefore, this choke-point tests the ability of the execution engine and the storage system to find an appropriate concurrency control technique to guarantee the consistency and efficiency. In particular, the transactions not only involve read-write operations on multiple entities but also require the MMDB to guarantee the consistency across the data model.

4.3   Example

To illustrate our choke-point-based design of queries, we take Query 5 (in Fig. 3) as an example to explain the technical challenge under the hood. Query 5 is that: *Given a start customer and a product category, find persons who are this customer's friends within 3-hop friendships in Knows graph, besides, they have bought products in the given category. Finally, return the feedback with the 5-rating review of those bought products.*

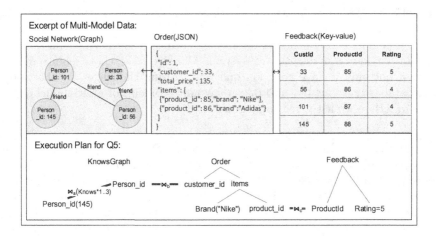

Fig. 3. Example of multi-model join

As Fig. 3 depicts, this query involves three data models: customer with 3-hop friends (*Graph*), order embedded with an item list (*JSON*), and customer's feedback (*Key-value*). From the business perspective, it can be used to explain the recommendation model for better transparency and user experience. From the technical dimension, there are three types of joins in the query: Graph-Graph ($\bowtie_a$), Graph-JSON ($\bowtie_b$) and JSON-KV ($\bowtie_c$) join. Nevertheless, as the order of filters and joins can affect the execution time, an important task for the query optimizer is to evaluate available plans and select the best one. Note that picking a wrong join order makes the performance drastically worse. For example, when there is no qualified tuple in the orders, traversing one thousand tuples in the graph and looking up thousands of key-value pairs would be a bad choice. A judicious way for this case is to filter the orders with given parameters, and avoid the graph traversal and index lookup for key-value pairs when there are no valid orders. Furthermore, Query 5 is challenging also because each model arises a cardinality estimation issue to the query optimizer, i.e., recursive path query for Graph, embedded array operation for JSON, and composite-key lookup for key-value.

5 Experiments

In this section, we report our experimental results, including the performance of data generation and the benchmark results. In the case of the setup, we generate the synthetic data on a cluster of three machines, each with double 4-core Xeon-E5540 CPU, 32 GB RAM, and 500 GB HDD. In addition, we conduct all benchmark experiments on another machine with double 6-core Xeon-E5649 CPU, 100 GB RAM, and 500 GB HDD. The client machine has a 4-core i5-4590 CPU with 16 GB RAM. We select two representative MMDBs: OrientDB and ArangoDB with community version 2.2.16 and 3.3.7. On the client-side, we develop a Node.js program integrated with each DB's official driver. All benchmark workloads are implemented in the program (except for the OrientDB transaction, which can only be fully supported using JAVA API at present).

5.1 Data Generation

Table 3 presents characteristics of three generated datasets, each of which consists of five data models. Unibench defines a set of scale factors (SFs), targeting systems of different sizes. The size of the resulting dataset is mainly affected by the number of persons (Relational entries). For benchmarking the databases, we leverage the data generator to produce three datasets with roughly size 1 GB, 10 GB, and 30 GB by using scale factors 1, 10, and 30, respectively. In the case of efficiency, experiment results suggest the data generator produced 1 GB and 10 GB multi-model datasets in 10 and 40 min, on our 8-core machine running MapReduce and Spark in "pseudo-distributed" mode. In terms of scalability, we successfully generate 30G multi-model data within 60 min on our three-node cluster.

Table 3. Characteristics of datasets.

SF	Generation time (min)	Number ($\times 10^4$) & size in megabytes				
		Relational entries	Key-value pairs	JSON objects	XML objects	Nodes and edges of graph
1	10	1.2 & 1.1	25.2 & 233.7	25.2 & 219.2	25.2 & 326.5	(123.1, 338.9) & 236.6
10	40	7.4 & 6.5	234.2 & 2313.1	234.2 & 2189.8	234.2 & 3568.6	(969.3, 3208.3) & 2095.8
30	60 (3 nodes)	18.3 & 15.8	636.8 & 6367.8	636.8 & 6184.9	636.8 & 11771.31	(2674.3, 10951.5) & 6191.5

5.2   Importing Time

We import three datasets, SF1, SF10, and SF30, into ArangoDB and OrientDB using command-line utilities *arangoimp* and *oetl*. Both are executed in a single thread. Since both of them have no native XML support, we skip the XML importing test (Note that one can also convert XML objects into JSON objects, but the method is simply similar to that for JSON documents). The importing time of key-value pairs is merged into the relational model's because both DBs employ the same import method. Regarding the additional cost for supporting join operations, OrientDB needs to create inverse links between relational and JSON data using *CREATE LINK* command. In comparison, there is no such cost for ArangoDB, because once the data is imported into the system, one can perform join queries immediately.

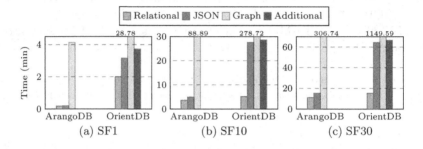

Fig. 4. Processing time for importing the multi-model datasets.

Figure 4 illustrates the result for loading three datasets. For better illustration, we measured the data loading time by four aspects, i.e., relational, JSON, graph, and additional cost. Overall, ArangoDB is 7.5x, 3.4x, and 3.8x faster than OrientDB for SF1, SF10, and SF30, respectively. Our observations are as follows. (i) For relational data, OrientDB is slightly slower as it takes time for creating unique *RID* to record the physical position for each row. On the contrary, ArangoDB employs original IDs as primary keys directly. (ii) For the JSON data, OrientDB has to transform each semi-structured JSON object into an *ODocument* object, while ArangoDB imports JSON data as *JSON lines format*, which allows it to load data in batches. (iii) For the graph data, OrientDB utilizes adjacency lists to store relations between all nodes. Thus an index lookup is needed when extracting every edge. In contrast, ArangoDB imports all edges into a *edge collection* as long as all imported documents have *_from* and *_to* attributes. This makes ArangoDB much faster than OrientDB for loading graph data. (iv) OrientDB requires additional cost for other tasks, e.g., creating links. Such cost increases drastically as data grows.

5.3   Performance of Multi-model Query

In this part, we issued ten multi-model queries on three datasets against ArangoDB and OrientDB. These queries are implemented using their query languages, i.e., *AQL* and *Orient SQL*. We use default indexes which are built on primary keys, and no secondary index is created. We provide the processing time of these queries in Fig. 5. We expect OrientDB could perform better at queries in the community level since these queries involve advanced graph traversal, but surprisingly, ArangoDB wins in most of the cases. This is due to its flexible data modeling, sophisticated query optimizer, and C++-implemented query function. Nevertheless, one exception is Q5 where OrientDB outperforms ArangoDB because the latter's query optimizer does not handle inner joins between graph and JSON efficiently, while OrientDB uses *composite SQL* queries to fetch correlated data from graph and JSON at the same time.

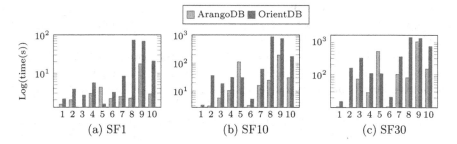

Fig. 5. Processing time on a logarithmic scale for queries, x-axis labels are query ids, i.e., Q1 to Q10.

5.4 Transaction Performance

We adopt Java and Node.js APIs which are only feasible ways at present to implement multi-model transactions for OrientDB and ArangoDB, respectively. This leads to two different patterns: synchronous processing for OrientDB, and asynchronous processing for ArangoDB. Similar to transactional operations in RDBMS, OrientDB utilizes *begin, rollback, commit* commands to proceed transactions. However, no such commands exist in ArangoDB. Instead, it executes a transaction via an *executeTransaction* JavaScript function. All involved data in the transaction needs to be declared beforehand.

Table 4. Throughput (transactions/second) of multi-model transactions

Database	Access method	Throughput for new order	Throughput for payment
ArangoDB	Asynchronous (Nodejs)	230.6	738.5
OrientDB	Synchronous (Java)	138.3	22.9

We ran two individual transactions (i.e., *New Order* and *Payment*) with a single thread for one minute, then compute the throughput per second. The operations of transactions in detail can be found in Table 2. Two DBs manage to *roll back* invalid transactions and *commit* valid ones, which means ACID properties on two multi-model transactions are guaranteed. Table 4 illustrates performances of both systems. The results indicate ArangoDB is better at write-heavy transaction (*Payment*) and OrientDB is more efficient in performing read-heavy transaction (*New order*). We believe this is due to the difference of their storage engines, i.e., LSM-tree-based storage for ArangoDB and B-tree-based storage for OrientDB.

6   Conclusion

Benchmarking multi-model databases is a challenging task since current public data and workloads can not well match various cases of applications. In this article, we introduce UniBench, a novel benchmark for multi-model databases. UniBench consists of a mixed data model, a scalable multi-model data generator, and a set of workloads including the multi-model aggregation, join, and transaction. Furthermore, we implement our proposed workloads on ArangoDB and OrientDB to illustrate the feasibility and usability of UniBench.

Several lessons are learned from the experimental study: (i) MMDBs are able to ingest a variety of data into storage without much additional efforts, (ii) MMDBs are able to support multi-model joins, such as graph-JSON, JSON-relational, and graph-relational. However, they lack specific algorithms to optimize the execution plan. (iii) MMDBs are able to support multi-entity and multi-model ACID transactions in the stand-alone mode, but the support for distributed ACID transactions remain on the future schedule.

As for future work, we would like to (i) introduce the flexibility into data generation because the data schema and data model in the real application could be changed dynamically, (ii) evaluate the performance of multi-model databases regarding different sharding strategies, and (iii) provide an open-source kit used to setup and run the benchmark, including the release of data generator and query implementations.

Acknowledgment. This work is partially supported by Academy of Finland (310321), China Scholarship (CSC) and CIMO Fellowship.

References

1. ArangoDB: Multi-model NoSQL database (2018). https://www.arangodb.com/
2. Carey, M.J., DeWitt, D.J., Naughton, J.F.: The OO7 benchmark. In: ACM SIG-MOD, pp. 12–21 (1993)
3. Chen, Y., et al.: A study of SQL-on-Hadoop systems. In: Big Data Benchmarks, Performance Optimization, and Emerging Hardware, pp. 154–166 (2014)
4. Cooper, B.F., Silberstein, A., Tam, E., Ramakrishnan, R., Sears, R.: Benchmarking cloud serving systems with YCSB. In: ACM SoCC, pp. 143–154 (2010)
5. DeWitt, D.J.: The Wisconsin benchmark: past, present, and future. In: The Benchmark Handbook, pp. 119–165 (1991)

6. Erling, O., et al.: The LDBC social network benchmark: interactive workload. In: SIGMOD (2015)
7. Fader, P.S.: Customer-base analysis with discrete-time transaction data. Ph.D. thesis, University of Auckland (2004)
8. Fader, P.S., Hardie, B.G., Lee, K.L.: RFM and CLV: using ISO-value curves for customer base analysis. J. Mark. Res. **42**(4), 415–430 (2005)
9. Feinberg, D., Adrian, M., Heudecker, N., Ronthal, A.M., Palanca, T.: Gartner magic quadrant for operational database management systems, 12 October 2015
10. Ghazal, A., et al.: BigBench: towards an industry standard benchmark for big data analytics. In: ACM SIGMOD (2013)
11. Gupta, S., et al.: Modeling customer lifetime value. J. Serv. Res. **9**(2), 139–155 (2006)
12. Huang, Z., Benyoucef, M.: From e-commerce to social commerce: a close look at design features. ECRA **12**, 246–259 (2013)
13. Lehmann, J., et al.: DBPedia - a large-scale, multilingual knowledge base extracted from Wikipedia. Semant. Web **6**(2), 167–195 (2015)
14. Leskovec, J., Adamic, L.A., Huberman, B.A.: The dynamics of viral marketing. TWEB **1**(1), 5 (2007)
15. Lu, J.: Benchmarking holistic approaches to XML tree pattern query processing. In: DASFAA Workshops, pp. 170–178 (2010)
16. Lu, J.: Towards benchmarking multi-model databases. In: CIDR (2017)
17. Lu, J., Holubová, I.: Multi-model data management: what's new and what's next? In: EDBT (2017)
18. Oliveira, F.R., del Val Cura, L.M.: Performance evaluation of NoSQL multi-model data stores in polyglot persistence applications. In: IDEAS, pp. 230–235 (2016)
19. OrientDB: Multi-model & graph database. http://orientdb.com/orientdb/
20. Pluciennik, E., Zgorzalek, K.: The Multi-model databases - a review. In: BDAS, pp. 141–152 (2017)
21. Poess, M., Rabl, T., Jacobsen, H., Caufield, B.: TPC-DI: the first industry benchmark for data integration. PVLDB **7**(13), 1367–1378 (2014)
22. Prat, A., Averbuch, A.: Benchmark design for navigational pattern matching benchmarking (2015). http://ldbcouncil.org/sites/default/files/LDBC_D3.3.34.pdf
23. Schmidt, A., Waas, F., Kersten, M.L., Carey, M.J., Manolescu, I., Busse, R.: XMark: a benchmark for XML data management. In: VLDB, pp. 974–985 (2002)
24. Stonebraker, M.: The case for polystores (2015). http://wp.sigmod.org/?p=1629
25. Transaction Processing Performance Council: TPC Benchmark C (Revision 5.11) (2010)
26. Wadsworth, E.: Buy'til you die-a walkthrough (2012)
27. Zhang, K.Z.: Consumer behavior in social commerce: a literature review. Decis. Support Syst. **86**, 95–108 (2016)

PolyBench: The First Benchmark for Polystores

Jeyhun Karimov[1]([✉]), Tilmann Rabl[1,2], and Volker Markl[1,2]

[1] DFKI, Kaiserslautern, Germany
jeyhun.karimov@dfki.de
[2] TU Berlin, Berlin, Germany

Abstract. Modern business intelligence requires data processing not only across a huge variety of domains but also across different paradigms, such as relational, stream, and graph models. This variety is a challenge for existing systems that typically only support a single or few different data models. Polystores were proposed as a solution for this challenge and received wide attention both in academia and in industry. These are systems that integrate different specialized data processing engines to enable fast processing of a large variety of data models. Yet, there is no standard to assess the performance of polystores. The goal of this work is to develop the first benchmark for polystores. To capture the flexibility of polystores, we focus on high level features in order to enable an execution of our benchmark suite on a large set of polystore solutions.

1 Introduction

Modern business questions frequently comprise complex analytical queries with multiple data types and data models, residing on several data storage and processing systems. This has led to a large number of domain-specific database engines with diverse capabilities since it is hard to support all kinds of heterogeneous queries within a single data processing engine [22]. For these setups, polystores have been proposed to combine systems that specialize in specific execution and data models.

Similarly, there is a growing community supporting one size might fit all, such as Apache Spark [27] and Weld [20]. These systems combine numerous analytics in a single engine to enable generic data representation and benefit from common intermediate representation for further optimization.

Despite the hype on heterogeneous analytics, whether on polystores or on single generic-purpose stores, there is no consistent evaluation method. As a result, each solution presents its own performance measurements. For example, some polystore solutions are built for a specific use-case [9], while others use TPC queries for their evaluation [12]. As a result, there is also no common workload, driver, and metrics for systems performing heterogeneous analytics. This makes it hard for a user to compare systems with different evaluation strategies. Although we concentrate on polystore evaluations in this paper, we also perform a thorough comparison between polystore and single, general-purpose engine.

© Springer Nature Switzerland AG 2019
R. Nambiar and M. Poess (Eds.): TPCTC 2018, LNCS 11135, pp. 24–41, 2019.
https://doi.org/10.1007/978-3-030-11404-6_3

We propose PolyBench, the first benchmark for heterogeneous analytics systems, especially for polystores, providing a complete evaluation environment. Our aim is to provide a benchmark suite with evaluation metrics and workloads, which will eventually lead to better baselines. Currently, a general accepted baseline for polystore evaluation is a single, general-purpose engine. The outcome of previous performance comparisons between polystores and single store engines is that polystores outperform single stores [7, 21]. However, as we show in this paper, this is not always the case. We evaluate the trade-offs between polystores and single-stores with various workloads.

PolyBench features a driver which benchmarks polystores with three main use-cases. We also provide a set of metrics which are specific to polystores. Our use-cases operate with structured, semi-structured, and unstructured data types and support relational, stream, array, and graph data processing paradigms. Our benchmark solution is not tied to a specific polystore solution, rather, it is generic and high level enough to be applied to any polystore.

We list the main contributions of this paper below:

– We propose PolyBench, the first polystore benchmark. Our benchmark suite consists of three main use-cases and two test scenarios. We provide a set of metrics for PolyBench, to conduct a thorough analysis.
– The main idea behind polystores is to overcome performance bottlenecks of single general-purpose stores. We conduct an analysis of this idea and compare polystores and single general-purpose stores.
– We conduct an extensive experimental analysis. We evaluate the systems under test with different parameters and combinations of parameters, provided by our benchmark driver.

We structure the rest of the paper as follows. We provide background information about the systems under test in Sect. 2. In Section 3, we survey related work. We explain use cases and our data model in Sect. 4. Section 5 describes test scenarios we adopt in PolyBench. We demonstrate our experimental analysis in Sect. 6. In Sect. 7, we discuss the results of experiments and analyze possible directions to improve our benchmark as future work. Finally, we conclude in Sect. 8.

2   Background

In this section, we give brief definitions of terms we utilize in this paper.

A **polystore** is union of different specialized stores, possibly with distinct language and execution semantics, supporting wide range of data types and analytics. We adopt the term polystore from BigDAWG [7]; however, our definition of polystore is more general to cover wide range of solutions. We utilize the term query for single stores and **use case** with polystores.

A **member-store** is a fundamental unit of a polystore, specialized and optimized for specific workloads. A member-store contributes most of its features to overall feature set of a polystore. As a result, a polystore supports a set of features and capabilities of its underlying member-stores. Once a user executes a use case to a polystore, a polystore optimizer splits the use case into subqueries, each of which directly addresses a particular member-store. A subquery might also contain embedded invocations to specified member-store's native query interface.

We differentiate three main member-stores. The first one is source member-store. A **source member-store** is a member-store from which a polystore ingests input data from outside world. The second one is sink member-store. A **sink member-store** is a member-store which reside in the last ring of the overall pipeline and provide the output of a given use case to the user. The third type is relay member-stores. A **relay member-store** is a member-store, except sink member-store, which ingests its input data from other member-stores.

In this paper, we consider a polystore as a blackbox and tune it only with high level APIs. For example, a connection between a member-store and a polystore, whether it is mediator-wrapper or grouped islands architecture, is a system-specific design decision and out of the scope of this paper.

A **single store** is a general-purpose store or engine, which might or might not be a specialized in one or many workloads, supporting various analytics. We adopt the term single store to differentiate it from member-stores. In our experimental setup a single store supports all required features to execute our workloads. This enables us to conduct a thorough analysis between single store and polystore.

3   Related Work

There is a large body of work on polystores, each of which features a unique evaluation technique. In this section, we give an overview of existing polystore evaluation techniques. Below we categorize related works based on their main focus.

Language. Language design is an important component of polystores. It hides complex systems programming from users. Bondiombouy et al. propose a functional SQL-like query language that integrates data retrieved from different data stores [4]. Kolev et al. propose a similar SQL-like approach [14]. The authors provide specific queries for an evaluation of their solution. However, the member-store for data placement and query execution is hardcoded in the queries. We, on the other hand, formulate our use cases for polystores to be transparent both in terms of data placement and engine selection.

Tools. To enable data transparency between member-stores of a polystore, efficient data transfer and transformations are required. Dziedzic et al. analyze data migration between a diverse set of databases, including PostgreSQL, SciDB, S-Store, and Accumulo [8]. Pipegen features a similar approach automatically generating data pipes between DBMSs [11]. The authors of both papers evaluate their solutions with data migration-/transformation-specific use cases. These benchmarks are difficult to generalize for polystore evaluation as they are not high level enough to cover a polystore benchmark.

Optimizer. Workflow optimization is important to efficiently place and move data in polystores. Chen et al. focus on the optimization of the amount of data movement [6,25]. The main limitation of this work is that data placement and member-stores are tightly coupled. Our benchmark on the other hand, has no prior assumption on data placement or migration. Because PolyBench considers systems under test as blackbox, our benchmark leaves all optimization decisions to the optimizer of a system under test. Jovanovic et al. soften the data placement condition in member-stores and develop an algorithm to choose member-stores [12]. The authors adopt TPC-H and TPC-DS queries for evaluation. MISO also adopts a similar evaluation method [15]. The main limitation is that TPC queries are not designed for heterogeneous analytics workloads.

Specialized Benchmarks. There are also some works focusing on polystore performance analysis. However, these typically consider only a specific polystore and analyze its capabilities. Kolev et al. analyze the polystore built on the CloudMdsQL language [14] and conduct experiments on the main features of relational and NoSQL engines [13]. Yu et al. evaluate the performance of BigDAWG [7] with MySQL and Vertica member-stores [26]. The authors adapt TPC-H queries for their evaluation. The main limitation of previous work is that the benchmark design is specific to the proposed solution. We, on the other hand, propose a generic benchmark suite that can be applied to any polystore solution.

Currently, BigDAWG executes workloads comprising diverse queries by identifying "sweet spots" in member-stores. However, to effectively identify strengths and weaknesses of query processing capabilities of member-stores, a formalization the performance characteristics is required. According to one of the authors of BigDAWG, Jennie Rogers, an important step to solve this problem is to find minimal set of evaluation use cases [2]. For a better performance, monitoring framework should feed the evaluation results to a polystore optimizer. Our work is the first initiative to solve the more general issue incorporating a diverse set of polystore solutions.

Lu et al. propose their vision to benchmark polystores concentrating on data models [17–19]. The main limitation of this proposal is that data model conversion and transformation is only one facet of general polystore evaluation. Furthermore, to ensure black-box evaluation, the data models and conversion between them should be transparent to the benchmark driver. Our benchmark suite, on the other hand, performs analysis in with high level APIs and leave all low-level details to system under test. BigBench is an industry standard benchmark for big data analytics [10]. The focus of this benchmark is benchmarking big data processing systems. We, on the other hand, concentrate on benchmarking polystores, combination of big data processing systems.

In previous works many different evaluation methods were proposed, each of which is specific to either one polystore instance or one implementation aspect. Our work is the first to propose a generic, holistic polystore benchmark.

4 Data Model and Use Case

PolyBench is an application level benchmark and simulates a banking business model. We choose banking, since it features heterogeneous analytics and data types. PolyBench's data set comprises structured, semi-structured, and unstructured parts.

4.1 Data Model

Relational. From the Fig. 1, ① describes the list of bank customers. ② is the list of people globally blacklisted. ③ is the customer transactions table.

Stream. The main characteristic of the stream data model is that data is continuously arriving, possibly infinitely. There is no standard streaming data format, it can be structured, semi-structured, and unstructured.

In Fig. 1 ④ is a stream that represents online operations. This is necessary for analyzing and debugging potential problems in real-time. One example would be real-time fraud detection. Another example is monitoring exchange operations and updating exchange rates based on the current assets of the bank.

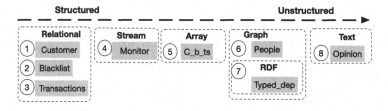

Fig. 1. PolyBench data model.

Array. While traditional DBMS platforms organize data in tables, array databases store data in array data model. The array model can have several dimensions, resulting in n-dimensional matrices. An array data model should be able to handle various scenarios, such as dense data (images), time series data, sparse arrays, and etc. The main goal is to fetch required data with few disk accesses by adjusting the tiling of the array to the access patterns. An array data model also tries to maintain a spatial proximity on disk, reducing the disk I/O during subsetting.

In Fig. 1 ⑤ shows our array data. We store 3-dimensional (customer - balance - time) data in an array format, which stores the balance of a customer at a given time.

Graph. Similar to stream data model, there is no unified way to represent graph data. We use two graph datasets for graph data. ⑥ represents the relationships between customers. This is useful for calculating credit scores of customers. If a customer has a financial connection with someone, that person's name can appear on customer credit report. As a result, when a bank looks to the customer credit report, it also checks people the customer linked with. Thus, having financial connections with people with low credit score can affect customer credit score. ⑦ shows the RDF data extracted from ⑥ and ⑧.

Text. Text data is an unstructured information that lacks a pre-defined data model. ⑧ includes comments or public tweets about a bank. We use publicly available customer review data set [16].

As we can see, the overall input data consists of different data models, each of which with a separate **homogeneous** data set. Throughout the paper we utilize the term **heterogeneous input** for the union of several **homogeneous inputs** to a system under test. For example, a heterogeneous input may consist of a set of relational, stream, and array homogeneous inputs.

4.2   Use Cases

The amount of data stored by banks is rapidly increasing triggering banks to push new data processing technologies into their production environment [23]. To survive in a competitive world, it is necessary to adopt big data analytics as part of their core data processing strategy Apart from the volume, the diversity of data also increases, resulting in heterogeneous data and processing models. Inspired by this trend, we provide three use cases in Figs. 2, 3 and 4.

```
INSERT INTO typed_dep VALUES (
CONVERT_INTO_RDF (
 SELECT *
 FROM Customer c
 WHERE c.updated >  arg  as u)
UNION
 CONVERT_INTO_RDF (
 SELECT *
 FROM People p
 WHERE p IN u)
UNION
 CONVERT_INTO_RDF (
 SELECT opinion_text
 FROM Opinion o
 WHERE o.ts > arg  )
)
```

Fig. 2. Use case 1

Bank Multi-model Data Integration. In this use case we combine data residing in different sources to provide users a unified view. We integrate ①,

```
SELECT *
FROM (
  SELECT customer.userID
  FROM customer
  WHERE cutomer.work = null) AS c,
  (SELECT userID
  FROM c_b_ts
  WHERE c_b_ts.balance > arg1
  AND c_b_ts.year=arg2) AS c2,
  (SELECT p.userID
  FROM people p
  WHERE p sp blacklisted < arg3)
  AS p

  WHERE p.userID = c.userID
  AND c.userID=c2.userID
```

Fig. 3. Use case 2

```
SELECT *
FROM customer c, transactions t, c_b_ts,
  (SELECT *
  FROM monitor m
  WHERE m.userID IN blacklist.userID)
  as fraud
  WHERE c.userID = fraud.userID
  AND t.userID = fraud.userID
  AND fraud.userID = c_b_ts.userID
  AND c_b_ts.ts within param_time
```

Fig. 4. Use case 3

⑥, and ⑧ into ⑦, constructing a clear high level abstraction. The use case utilizes RDF as a target data type. At the sink operator of each engine, except the sink member-store, we put an additional operator, CONVERT_INTO_RDF. The operator converts relational data (Customer table) to RDF (id - columnName - columnValue). The conversion of graph data model is in (sourcePersonID - relationName - destPersonID) format. For the text data, we extract (object - predicate - subject) patterns and construct RDF[1].

Customer Background Check. In this use case we check customer background to detect suspicious customers for further investigation. Schufa[2] is one example for customer background check. In our use case, if a customer is unemployed but has last year overall balance above some threshold and has very few connections to other people (for people having accounts in offshore banks)

---

[1] We partially benefitted from the library https://github.com/codemaniac/sopex.

[2] https://www.schufa.de.

or some connections to blacklisted people, then the use case takes them into further consideration.

Continuous Queries: Fraud Detection. In many financial applications, a data processing system may consume data in the form of continuous data streams, rather than finite stored data set. In this use case we consume and process realtime data and enrich it with other data sources. To be more precise, for every streaming tuple from (4) we check if the tuple ID is blacklisted. If so, we retrieve all transactions and balance information for the last week for the particular user for further investigation.

Based on the physical query execution plan of a polystore we categorize our use cases into two groups: dependent and independent polystore use cases. A **dependent polystore use case** is a use case, which consists of at least one relay member-store as a result of polystore deployment plan. An **independent polystore use case** is a use case which does not have any relay member-store as a result of a polystore deployment plan.

5   Benchmark Design

5.1   Metrics

Metrics are standard units to measure the performance of a system under test. Previous works generally adopt runtime as main metric for polystores. Although this is a proper metric for a polystore evaluation, it is not enough to get a good overview of polystore performance. Below we provide a set of metrics that we adopt for our benchmark.

Runtime. We use the term runtime for test scenarios consisting of batch use cases. Runtime is the time span between the polystore's start time, earliest start time of the member-stores, and end time, the latest end-time of member-stores, for processing the given use case. Thus, runtime is associated with the whole polystore system.

We use the term latency for interactive test scenarios consisting of continuous and batch use cases. We compute latency metric per tuple. The latency is the time span between tuple entering the source member-store and the related result emission time from sink member-store.

Individual Runtime. Although we are interested mainly in the overall runtime of a use case, to perform a thorough analysis it is important to measure individual runtimes of subqueries running in different member-stores. Individual runtime is the runtime of each member-store in a polystore. We adopt the term individual latency for use cases containing continuous test scenarios.

Idle Time. The above metrics are related to the time span in which a polystore or a member-store performs data processing. However, member-stores might stay idle for some use cases. The idle time is a time span in which a member-store does not perform any computation. The reason is mainly a blocking upstream member-store, especially in dependent polystore use cases. Note that only elected member-stores, which are selected by polystore query optimizer for executing a given use case, are considered for this metric.

Load. In PolyBench the load is defined by the size of the heterogeneous input data. We adopt 10 GB, 50 GB, and 100 GB heterogeneous input data each of which consists of different homogeneous input data sizes.

5.2   Test Scenarios

Our test scenarios categorize the use cases based on their mode, which can be (i) one-shot scenarios, (ii) continuous scenarios. We propose two main test scenarios for PolyBench. In our experiments, we analyze each test scenario separately and together. Because there are many parameters contributing to the performance of a polystore, we design our test scenarios to measure the best and the worst performance after parameter tuning.

Resource Distribution. The first test scenario is resource distribution among member-stores. Member-stores reside in the left set and resources are in the right set. There is a many-to-many relation between the two sets. In this test scenario, we evaluate the result of different mapping strategies from member-stores set to resources set.

The resource distribution scenario receives the amount of overall resources as an input. In our case the resource includes nodes in a cluster, memory, and CPU. The test scenario assigns each resource to a particular member-store and ensures all resources are utilized by member-stores of a polystore. For the single store case, it assigns all resources to the resource manager of the single store engine.

One usage of this test scenario is scale-out/in scenarios. For example, a user has some information about the input data. She knows with the existing resources it is inefficient to process all of input data. So, once a user decides to add new resources, because of the performance issues, a polystore should distribute new resources among member-stores in an optimal way.

Load Distribution. The second test scenario is load distribution among member-stores. There are two main factors contributing to the load of member-stores, being an input data size and assigned subqueries. Suppose a user submits a use case to a polystore. The polystore optimizer divides the use case to several subqueries, based on some meta-data and assigns subqueries to member-stores. As a result of the assignment if the performance of a particular member-store is a bottleneck to the whole use case, then there are several solutions. One option is to share the subquery with another member-store, which also supports all necessary features to execute the subquery. Another option is to recompile the use case and reassign subqueries to member-stores.

Because subquery assignment to member-stores is an internal process of a system under test and because we treat system under test as a blackbox, we concentrate on the second factor contributing the load distribution test scenario, being an input data size. Because the heterogeneous input consists of different homogeneous inputs, the idea of this test scenario is to tune the size of homogeneous inputs, find different ratio of homogeneous input sizes and ensure the size of heterogeneous input data is constant.

6 Experiments

6.1 Setup

We conduct experiments with the polystore BigDAWG v0.1 and single general purpose engine Apache Spark v2.3.0. We use Apache Giraph v1.2.0 [3] for workloads containing graph processing. We setup our experiments on a shared-nothing cluster. Our cluster consists of 20 nodes. Each node is equipped with 2.40 GHz Intel(R) Xeon(R) CPU with 16 cores. System clocks in all machines throughout the cluster are synchronized via a local NTP server. Unless stated otherwise, we deploy all member-stores of a polystore to different cluster nodes. We utilize 10 GB, 50 GB, and 100 GB datasets for benchmarking.

6.2 Use Case 1

We convert each tuple to RDF format in the sink operator of member-stores. Analyzing the deployment plan of BigDAWG we conclude that the use case belongs to the dependent polystore queries. To be more precise, the result of select operation from the People table depends on the output of the select operation from the Customer table. As a result, the latter is a blocking operation for the former.

As we discussed in Sect. 5, the input data distribution contributes to the member-store load. In the following experiment, we keep the deployment configurations of BigDAWG constant and change the size/ratio of homogeneous input data keeping the overall heterogeneous input data size constant. The idea of the use case is that an enterprise might lack prior knowledge of the statistics of input data sets.

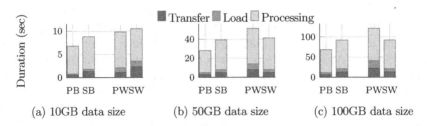

(a) 10GB data size   (b) 50GB data size   (c) 100GB data size

Fig. 5. Effect of tuning homogeneous data sizes with 10 GB, 50 GB, and 100 GB heterogeneous input data size. PB stands for BigDAWG performance with tuned data distribution, SB stands for Spark performance with tuned data distribution (the same distribution as PB), PW stands for the worst BigDAWG performance, and SW means Spark performance with homogeneous input data same distribution as PW.

Figure 5 shows the effect of different homogeneous input data sizes, keeping the heterogeneous data size constant, for systems under test. We consider two cases: (*i*) the best case - input data distribution is tuned according to deployment of member-stores and (*ii*) the worst case - the distribution of input data and member-stores deployment are uncorrelated. In the first case, we tune the homogeneous input data sizes to be executed by different member-stores to maximize to overall performance of BigDAWG. In the second case, we show the worst performance of BigDAWG. In both experiments we also evaluate the single general purpose store. We observe that once we tune the ratio of homogeneous inputs, then BigDAWG performs better than Spark, because each member-store is specialized for special workloads and we provide such a particular workload.

We can see in Fig. 5 that Spark is more robust to the changes in input data set, than BigDAWG. The reason is that Spark utilizes all dedicated resources, as opposed to a member-store which utilizes only a portion of the resources dedicated to BigDAWG. As a result, a member-store is more prone to become a bottleneck (to the whole polystore) than Spark. Indeed, if there are more bottleneck member-stores, then the overall performance of a polystore degrades significantly.

We also observe a serious performance degradation for BigDAWG once we play with the amount of homogeneous input data. Moreover, with increasing heterogeneous data size, the gap between the best and the worst case increases as well. One reason behind this behavior is scheduling. In BigDAWG a member-store can belong to only one island, although it might feature several characteristics of different islands. As a result, the BigDAWG scheduler is unable to share a subquery to member-stores residing in different islands. This causes limitations when the size of one homogeneous input data is larger than others.

In Spark, data sources reside in the upstream of the source operator. The source operators receive data from external data sources while other operators pull input data from upstream operators. When there is a blocking operation in the upstream operator, the global scheduler of Spark, DAGScheduler, assigns a non-blocking task to downstream task schedulers. The global scheduler might also eliminate downstream operator for some time allocating more resources to blocking upstream operator.

Similarly, in BigDAWG source member-stores receive input from external data sources and other member-stores obtain input data from upstream member-stores. The main limitation is that BigDAWG scheduler is not as dynamic as Spark scheduler. As a result, especially for dependent polystore use cases, an upstream member-store can easily become a bottleneck. That is, the result of the selection query in People table depends on the result of the selection query from Customer table. As a result, member-store associated with the former table stays idle until the member-store linked with the latter table finishes. The problem increases with larger input data sizes.

Another reason behind poor performance, we observe in Fig. 5, of BigDAWG with non-tuned data distribution is data partitioning. For a single system selecting an optimal data partitioning is a non-trivial task [24]. Performing so for a polystore is more challenging task as the task includes (*i*) partitioning data among member-stores and (*ii*) partitioning data within separate member-stores.

BigDAWG setup's transfer and load times contribute significantly to the overall use case runtime. The impact increases with increasing input data size. The main reason is that efficient data transfer strategies between different member-stores requires n-to-m connections between one member-store with n instances and another one with m instances. This is non-trivial as it requires changing an engine's communication internals and can cause synchronization issues. In Spark, on the other hand, these details are automatically handled transparent to a user.

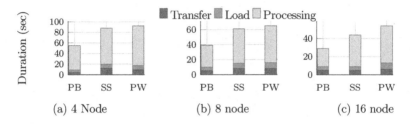

(a) 4 Node   (b) 8 node   (c) 16 node

Fig. 6. Effect of scaling out in Spark and BigDAWG with 4, 8, and 16-node configurations. PB stands for the best performance of scaling out BigDAWG, SS means scaling out Spark, and PW mean the worst performance for scaling out BigDAWG.

Figure 6 shows the main idea behind scaling out in BigDAWG and Spark environment. In this case, we fix both heterogeneous and homogeneous data size and consider the number nodes in cluster as a variable. As a result, a user should be able to benefit from the performance of the systems under test with adding more resources. In this case we accept heterogeneous and homogeneous data as a constant variable.

We can observe that once a user has knowledge about the input data domain and engine characteristics of the member-stores, then tuning BigDAWG for scaling out results with the best performance compared to Spark. Engine characteristics of member-stores refers to an estimation of each member-store performance with more resources.

We see a consistent scale-out performance for Spark. As we add more nodes to the cluster, the duration of computation improves. Although there are several parameters to tune manually such as garbage collection, serialized RDD storage, level of parallelism, and memory usage of reduce tasks, Spark performs the main network and I/O tuning transparent to the user. From this perspective, the required systems expertise is less for tuning the single engine for scaling out.

We note that the worst case scaling out scenario for BigDAWG causes performance problems. Worst case scaling out occurs when we increase the amount of resources to a set of member-stores without having enough information about the characteristics of member-stores. A lightweight monitoring system, which

BigDAWG currently lacks, might be a solution for this problem, where the framework monitors the performance of operators inside member-stores and member-stores as a whole and feed the information to the optimizer which assigns available resources among member-stores and among instances of particular member-store in an optimal way.

Although benchmarking scenarios individually is important, testing the performance of systems under test with combinations of different test scenarios gives us more insights. In Figure 7, we benchmark the performance of the systems under test with combination of both test scenarios: resource distribution and load distribution. The scenario occurs when a user is not an expert in Big-DAWG and there is a little knowledge about input data. The result is that the performance gap between BigDAWG and Spark increases more than in the above experiments.

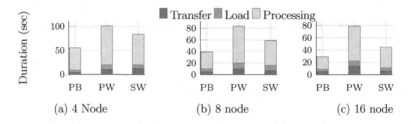

Fig. 7. Effect of scaling with different homogeneous data distribution for BigDAWG and Spark. PB stands for the best performance for BigDAWG. PW stands for the worst BigDAWG performance. SW stands for the performance of Spark. The heterogeneous input data size is constant.

6.3   Use Case 2

From the deployment plan of BigDAWG, we note that Use Case 2 is an independent polystore use case. BigDAWG divides the use case into sub-queries, submits to the relevant member-stores and merges once the results of all member-stores are ready. Independent polystore use cases spend less time for data transformation (from one member-store format to another) and reduce the amount of idle stay waiting for an upstream member-store.

We analyze the load distribution test scenario with BigDAWG and compare it with Spark. Figure 8 shows the results of engine load for Use Case 2. Idle time is the sum of periods in which member-stores stay idle. For the equal load in the figure, we configure member-stores such that the overall idle time is minimized. For skewed load, on the other hand, we arrange the distribution of the load to be random and to be different from each other at least 20%.

We observe that with a shared load, BigDAWG performs better than Spark. In this experiment, we measure the performance of a member-store with different loads and select a load combination which ensures the best performance for the

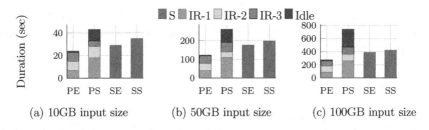

(a) 10GB input size   (b) 50GB input size   (c) 100GB input size

Fig. 8. Effect of engine load. PE refers to BigDAWG with equal load for member-stores, PS refers to BigDAWG with skewed load, SE refers to Spark with same load as PE, and SS refers to the performance of Spark with the same load as PS. Legends: S refers to runtime of Spark, IR-n refers to the individual runtime of nth member-store, and Idle refers to the overall idle time of BigDAWG.

whole polystore. The main reason behind the better performance of BigDAWG with shared load is that each member-store is specialized in assigned workload, resulting in overall improved performance.

We also perform experiment with skewed load. As a result, we can observe significantly increased idle times. Moreover, as the data size increases, the impact of idle time increases. We also observe a correlation between runtime of an individual member-stores and idle time.

We can also see that Spark is less susceptible to skewed load than Big-DAWG. The reason is better scheduling and adaptive resource allocation in Spark. Dynamic resource allocation and scheduling is simpler in single engine environment. As a result, idle time duration in a cluster and the impact of skew is minimized in Spark. To avoid data skew, Spark, adopts TreeReduce and TreeAggregate methods and new aggregation communication pattern based on multi-level aggregation trees. At the beginning of the job, Spark's DAGScheduler assigns task schedulers to combine partial aggregates on local executors. Then, Spark shuffles the locally aggregated data to pre-scheduled reducers. For BigDAWG case, on the other hand, the optimizer lacks similar features, which in turn results in relatively poor performance.

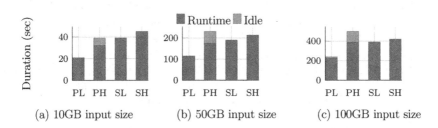

(a) 10GB input size   (b) 50GB input size   (c) 100GB input size

Fig. 9. Effect of engine selectivity for BigDAWG and Spark. PL stands for BigDAWG with low selective subqueries, PH means BigDAWG with high selective subqueries, SL stands for Spark with low selective operators, and SH means Spark with high selective operators.

Similarly, in Fig. 9 we analyze the effect of subquery selectivity in BigDAWG and operator selectivity in Spark. We define low selectivity being $s \leq 0.2$ and high selectivity being $s \geq 0.8$.

6.4   Use Case 3

Figure 10 shows the latency of input tuples. We can observe the skew in the latency distribution among member-stores. For example, the streaming engine in BigDAWG has the lowest latency. Because relational and array databases in our polystore are not optimized for streaming workloads, we observe a relatively high latency for the particular member-stores. Another reason for this behavior is synchronization and scheduling overhead among member-stores. For this type of queries BigDAWG would have benefited from caching feature among member-stores. Spark, on the other hand, provides automatic caching of frequently used RDDs.

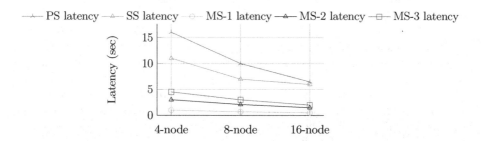

Fig. 10. Effect of running continuous queries on BigDAWG and Spark. PS latency stands for the latency of BigDAWG , SS latency means the latency of Spark, MS-1 is S-Store, MS-2 is PostgreSQL and MS-3 is SciDB.

We notice that the input/output semantics of member-stores is prone to be a bottleneck, especially with workloads including continuous queries. For example, the streaming member-store adopts a pull-based approach to ingest the input data and push based approach to output. It is not desirable to accumulate data inside the engine because once an operator state gets bigger, the performance degrades. For relational databases the input/output semantics are more relaxed. Depending on the size of the output, the system can stream or save the data in a temporary table for later use. Because backpressure mechanism is not available in polystores, adding flow controls to each engine, causes an additional latency because of the synchronization overhead among member-stores.

7   Discussion and Future Work

In this section, we summarize the findings of our experimental results. There is a need for better query optimizers and automation tools for polystores. Although this is not a new area in database research, existing optimizers work best for

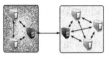   

(a) A polystore data exchange via direct socket.   (b) A polystore data exchange through disc.   (c) A polystore data exchange via intermediate system.   (d) Data transfer for single store.

Fig. 11. Data transfer strategies for polystore and single store.

a specific set of workloads. The overhead and required knowledge for tuning polystores is considerably higher than single store engines. Tuning a system is important to optimize and homogenize the performance. Although there is a large amount of research on self-tuning systems [5], performing so for a single-store system is still non-trivial. However, having information about input data can ease the work of database admin significantly. Tuning polystores for a given workload is much harder problem than tuning a single store systems. Tuning a polystore includes tuning all member-stores individually. Moreover, once there is a correlation among member-store workloads, as we saw in our experiments, tuning a polystore becomes even more complicated. For example, if the query involves interchanging the data between member-stores, the exact tuning decision is non-trivial at compile time.

A two-level scheduler (local for member-store and global for polystore) leads to non-negligible idle times. Relaxing the border between different layers of schedulers would increase polystore performance considerably.

In our experiments, we notice data representation and transfer to be a significant issue. While some works [11,20] use a single data representation [1], others have multiple data representation [7]. The same is true for data transfer. Especially for continuous queries data transfer layers can easily become a bottleneck. The reason is that backpressure is non-trivial to implement for polystores, which would lead to gathering massive amounts of data in data transfer layer. Figure 11 shows three possible data transfer strategies for polystores and the data transfer for a single store. Although all different strategies have their own advantages and limitations, selecting the best option for the given workload is essential to improve the performance of polystores. BigDAWG, for example, supports the transfer strategies depicted in Figs. 11a and b; however, these are hardcoded in the implementation and, thus, are not considered as a variable for an optimizer.

8   Conclusion

Polystores are designed to overcome the limitations of single general purpose data stores. To fill various gaps in data processing, there is an increasing number of polystores, with member-stores featuring different data models and execution models. This makes the solutions challenging to benchmark. In this paper we present PolyBench, the first benchmark for polystores. Our benchmark is generic and high level to support wide range of existing polystore solutions. We conduct an experimental analysis on a single store and a polystore and provide a comparative analysis. Our key finding is that, although polystores are a key solution for most enterprise use cases, there are significant limitations for evaluation in previous works. Firstly, polystores perform better with tuned load and resource distribution. Secondly, current polystore designs are not compatible with continuous queries. We identify the main reasons for the above behaviours as lack of advanced optimizer, scheduler, and data transfer layer.

Considering that this work proposes the first benchmark for polystores, there is still a research to be carried for a complete and standard benchmark. A useful extension to our benchmark would be to support specialized polystores. Examples are graph based polystores and ML based polystores. An improvement would be to add workloads with all possible combinations of the above. An extension for measuring individual components would be to support benchmarking polystore tools, such as data transfer and data representation tools. Moreover, important metrics such as ease of use, maintainability, high availability, and performance robustness are key in production environment, which is part of the future work.

Acknowledgments. This work has been supported by the European Commission through Proteus (ref. 687691) and Streamline (ref. 688191) and by the German Ministry for Education and Research as Berlin Big Data Center BBDC (funding mark 01IS14013A).

References

1. Apache Arrow: a cross-language development platform for in-memory data. https://arrow.apache.org/. Accessed 24 Feb 2018
2. Query modeling and optimization in the BigDAWG polystore system. http://istc-bigdata.org/index.php/query-modeling-and-optimization-in-the-bigdawg-polystore-system/. Accessed 10 Mar 2018
3. Avery, C.: Giraph: large-scale graph processing infrastructure on Hadoop. In: Proceedings of the Hadoop Summit, Santa Clara, vol. 11, pp. 5–9 (2011)
4. Bondiombouy, C., Kolev, B., Levchenko, O., Valduriez, P.: Integrating big data and relational data with a functional SQL-like query language. In: Chen, Q., Hameurlain, A., Toumani, F., Wagner, R., Decker, H. (eds.) DEXA 2015. LNCS, vol. 9261, pp. 170–185. Springer, Cham (2015). https://doi.org/10.1007/978-3-319-22849-5_13
5. Chaudhuri, S., Narasayya, V.: Self-tuning database systems: a decade of progress. In: Proceedings of the 33rd International Conference on Very Large Data Bases, pp. 3–14. VLDB Endowment (2007)
6. Chen, Y., Xu, C., Rao, W., Min, H., Su, G.: Octopus: hybrid big data integration engine. In: 2015 IEEE 7th International Conference on Cloud Computing Technology and Science (CloudCom), pp. 462–466. IEEE (2015)
7. Duggan, J., et al.: The BigDAWG polystore system. ACM SIGMOD Rec. **44**(2), 11–16 (2015)
8. Dziedzic, A., Elmore, A.J., Stonebraker, M.: Data transformation and migration in polystores. In: 2016 IEEE High Performance Extreme Computing Conference (HPEC), pp. 1–6. IEEE (2016)

9. Gadepally, V., et al.: The BigDAWG polystore system and architecture. In: 2016 IEEE High Performance Extreme Computing Conference (HPEC), pp. 1–6. IEEE (2016)
10. Ghazal, A., et al.: BigBench: towards an industry standard benchmark for big data analytics. In: Proceedings of the 2013 ACM SIGMOD International Conference on Management of Data, pp. 1197–1208. ACM (2013)
11. Haynes, B., Cheung, A., Balazinska, M.: PipeGen: data pipe generator for hybrid analytics. In: Proceedings of the Seventh ACM Symposium on Cloud Computing, pp. 470–483. ACM (2016)
12. Jovanovic, P., Simitsis, A., Wilkinson, K.: Engine independence for logical analytic flows. In: 2014 IEEE 30th International Conference on Data Engineering (ICDE), pp. 1060–1071. IEEE (2014)
13. Kolev, B., Pau, R., Levchenko, O., Valduriez, P., Jiménez-Peris, R., Pereira, J.: Benchmarking polystores: the cloudMdsQL experience. In: 2016 IEEE International Conference on Big Data (Big Data), pp. 2574–2579. IEEE (2016)
14. Kolev, B., Valduriez, P., Bondiombouy, C., Jiménez-Peris, R., Pau, R., Pereira, J.: CloudMdsQL: querying heterogeneous cloud data stores with a common language. Distrib. Parallel Databases **34**(4), 463–503 (2016)
15. LeFevre, J., Sankaranarayanan, J., Hacigumus, H., Tatemura, J., Polyzotis, N., Carey, M.J.: MISO: souping up big data query processing with a multistore system. In: Proceedings of the 2014 ACM SIGMOD International Conference on Management of Data, pp. 1591–1602. ACM (2014)
16. Leskovec, J., Sosič, R.: SNAP: a general-purpose network analysis and graph-mining library. ACM Trans. Intell. Syst. Technol. (TIST) **8**(1), 1 (2016)
17. Lu, J.: Towards benchmarking multi-model databases. In: CIDR (2017)
18. Lu, J., Holubová, I.: Multi-model data management: what's new and what's next? In: EDBT, pp. 602–605 (2017)
19. Lu, J., Liu, Z.H., Xu, P., Zhang, C.: UDBMS: road to unification for multi-model data management. arXiv preprint arXiv:1612.08050 (2016)
20. Palkar, S., et al.: Weld: a common runtime for high performance data analytics. In: Conference on Innovative Data Systems Research (CIDR) (2017)
21. Simitsis, A., Wilkinson, K., Castellanos, M., Dayal, U.: Optimizing analytic data flows for multiple execution engines. In: Proceedings of the 2012 ACM SIGMOD International Conference on Management of Data, pp. 829–840. ACM (2012)
22. Stonebraker, M., Cetintemel, U.: "One size fits all": an idea whose time has come and gone. In: Proceedings of 21st International Conference on Data Engineering, ICDE 2005, pp. 2–11. IEEE (2005)
23. Sun, N., Morris, J., Xu, J., Zhu, X., Xie, M.: ICARE: a framework for big data-based banking customer analytics. IBM J. Res. Dev. **58**(5/6), 4:1–4:9 (2014)
24. Valduriez, P.: Parallel database systems: open problems and new issues. Distrib. Parallel Databases **1**(2), 137–165 (1993)
25. Xu, C., Chen, Y., Liu, Q., Rao, W., Min, H., Su, G.: A unified computation engine for big data analytics. In: 2015 IEEE/ACM 2nd International Symposium on Big Data Computing (BDC), pp. 73–77. IEEE (2015)
26. Yu, K., Gadepally, V., Stonebraker, M.: Database engine integration and performance analysis of the BigDAWG polystore system. In: 2017 IEEE High Performance Extreme Computing Conference (HPEC), pp. 1–7. IEEE (2017)
27. Zaharia, M., Chowdhury, M., Franklin, M.J., Shenker, S., Stoica, I.: Spark: cluster computing with working sets. In: HotCloud, vol. 10, no. 10–10, p. 95 (2010)

Benchmarking Distributed Data Processing Systems for Machine Learning Workloads

Christoph Boden[1,2(✉)], Tilmann Rabl[1,2], Sebastian Schelter[1,2], and Volker Markl[1,2]

[1] Technische Universität Berlin, Berlin, Germany
{christoph.boden,tilmann.rabl,sebastian.schelter, volker.markl}@tu-berlin.de
[2] DFKI, Kaiserslautern, Germany

Abstract. Distributed data processing systems have been widely adopted to robustly scale out computations on massive data sets to many compute nodes in recent years. These systems are also popular choices to scale out the training of machine learning models. However, there is a lack of benchmarks to assess how efficiently data processing systems actually perform at executing machine learning algorithms at scale. For example, the learning algorithms chosen in the corresponding systems papers tend to be those that fit well onto the system's paradigm rather than state of the art methods. Furthermore, experiments in those papers often neglect important aspects such as addressing all aspects of scalability. In this paper, we share our experience in evaluating novel data processing systems and present a core set of experiments of a benchmark for distributed data processing systems for machine learning workloads, a rationale for their necessity as well as an experimental evaluation.

1 Introduction

Over the last years, we have observed a massive increase of available data. Due to rapidly falling storage costs, the ominpresence of online web applications and smart phones, text, audio, and video data as well as user interaction logs are being gathered at impressive scale. These have successfully been leveraged to build and significantly improve data-driven applications [35] and bossted scientific research. With this data, it became feasible to test hypotheses on data sets that are several orders of magnitude larger than before.

In light of the massive data sets being amassed, distributed data processing systems commonly referred to as "Big Data Analytics" systems have been developed in order to scale out computations and analysis to such massive data set sizes. The availability of massive data sets and these data processing systems together with machine learning algorithms have enabled remarkable improvements for a number of important tasks such as ranking web search results [12,23] or personalized content recommendation [22,37]. In this context, tt has

© Springer Nature Switzerland AG 2019
R. Nambiar and M. Poess (Eds.): TPCTC 2018, LNCS 11135, pp. 42–57, 2019.
https://doi.org/10.1007/978-3-030-11404-6_4

been observed that given enough data, comparatively simple algorithms could deliver superior performance to more complex and mathematically sophisticated approaches [31]. This observation and the ubiquity of data sets set of an unprecedented rise in demand for efficiently executing machine learning algorithms at scale. It quickly became clear that the main representative of these new distributed data processing systems, Hadoop MapReduce, was inadequate for such workloads, as it was inherently inefficient at their execution [36,49]. This led to very active research and development of new systems and paradigms addressing these drawbacks in distributed systems and database systems research communities [13,25,26,42,54].

But while the corresponding systems papers showed that these systems outperform Hadoop for certain iterative algorithms [5,41,54], it remains to be shown how efficiently they actually perform at executing machine learning algorithms at scale. On the one hand, the iterative algorithms chosen in the corresponding systems papers were mostly learning algorithms that are well suited for the underlying system paradigm rather than state of the art methods (e.g. gradient boosted trees) which would be the preferred choice for a supervised learning problem without the presence of such systems' constraints and are likely to provide superior prediction quality.

While existing Benchmarks for the performance evaluation of relational database systems for transactional workloads (TPC-C) and OLAP workloads (TPC-H) are widely accepted in industry and academia alike, the benchmarking landscape for distributed data processing systems is by no means as mature. Efforts in the benchmarking community, notably TPCx-HS and TPCx-BB [6,28] focused on evaluating these systems for the use case they were originally designed for: robustly scaling out simple computations and transformations to massive data sets. There is a need for a Benchmark to adequately assess the performance of scaling out machine learning workloads on data processing systems, consisting of an objective set of workloads, experiments and metrics.

Contribution: In this paper we share our experience in evaluating novel data processing systems for scalable machine learning workloads and outline the requirements, intricacies and pitfalls that one encounters when developing a benchmark for this scenario. Based on these insights, we specify what we deem to be a core set of experiments that constitute a benchmark for distributed data processing systems for scalable machine learning workloads and provide a rationale for their necessity.

The remainder of the paper is structured as follows: first we provide a brief overview of the machine learning workloads in Sect. 2. Subsequently we discuss the intricacies of evaluating machine learning workloads an the need to explore the model quality and runtime performance trade-off for distributed and single machine implementations of machine learning algorithms. In Sect. 4 we discuss the different aspects of scalability in the context of benchmarking distributed dataflow systems for machine learning workloads and subsequently conclude the paper.

2   Machine Learning for Data Processing Systems

The machine learning methods of interest in the context of distributed data processing systems can be categorized into three major groups: *Clustering*, *Classification* and *Recommender Systems*. We will briefly introduce the notation and representative algorithms chosen for our proposed benchmark experiments in this Section. As a first pre-processing step, before the actual machine learning algorithms can be applied, the raw data has to be transformed into a numeric representation usually called *features* through so-called *feature extraction*. When working with data from large-scale web applications, this processes consists of acquiring, parsing and integrating huge log-files or raw text obtained from the world wide web. The ultimate goal beeing the transformation of this data into numerical feature values in the form of feature vectors $x = (x_1, \ldots x_n)^T$. This pre-processing step is undoubtedly a good fit for parallel execution on distributed data processing systems. The usually very large raw data set sizes of input data sets as well as the simplicity of the necessary transformations and aggregations being applied to distill the feature vectors are exactly what these systems where designed and built for. After processing the entirety of the input data, the resulting *training data set* is generally represented by a numerical data matrix $X \in \mathrm{I\!R}^{(n \times d)}$ consisting of all n training data points with a feature space dimensionality d each.

2.1   Clustering (Unsupervised Learning)

A common task facing un-categorized data is to group data points into clusters according to inherent structure in the data set. Such a clustering may provide insight into the data by itself or serve as a input to further analysis or machine learning tasks downstream. Given a data matrix $A \in \mathrm{I\!R}^{(n \times d)}$ without any associated label or class information, the task in *unsupervised learning* or *clustering* is to partition the data into subsets (or *clusters*) such that all elements within one cluster are as similar as possible to each other yet as dissimilar as possible to other clusters according to some particular similarity metric.

As a representative workload we propose the use of the popular algorithm for clustering called *k-means*, which minimizes the intra-cluster distances between the data points x_i in a cluster j and it's center (or *centroid*) μ_j: by solving the following objective:

$$\min \sum_{j=1}^{k} \sum_{i \in C_j} ||x_i - \mu_j||^2$$

over the training data set X. The algorithm requires a Euclidean space and that the number of clusters k is chosen a priori. The *k-means* algorithm solves the optimization problem with the following heuristic: first, k cluster centers are initially sampled from the data set, next, the euclidean distance to each of these so called *centroids* is computed for every data point and finally every data point is assigned to its closest centroid and thus a cluster. After this assignment, new centroids are computed using the average of all cluster points. This iterates until convergence.

2.2 Classification (Supervised Learning)

Contrary to the unsupervised learning setting, the main problem in *supervised learning* is to fit a function $f : X \rightarrow Y$ that accurately predicts a label $y \in Y$ for unseen data points based on a set of training samples $(x_i, y_i) \in X \times Y$. More concretely, the objective of a classification algorithm is to learn a function

$$f : \mathbb{R}^N \rightarrow \{0, 1\}$$

that accurately predicts the labels y on previously unseen data points. The core task of a supervised learning algorithm is thus to fit the parameters (also called *model weights*) w of this function $f_w : X \rightarrow Y$ leveraging the training data and a so-called *loss function* $l : Y \times Y \rightarrow \mathbb{R}$ which encodes the fit between the known label y and the function prediction $f_w(x)$. To avoid that the function simply learns idiosyncrasies of the input data rather than generalize well to unseen data points, a so-called regularization term $\Omega(w)$ that encodes the complexity of the model is often simply added to the objective (e.g. the L_1 or L_2 norm of w). With this addition, the canonical supervised learning optimization problem is given by:

$$\hat{w} = argmin_w \left(\sum_{(x,y)\in(X,Y)} l\left(f_w\left(x\right), y\right) + \lambda \cdot \Omega\left(w\right) \right)$$

Contrary to traditional optimization problems, the optimization of this objective is carried out on on a separate training data set that already has the corresponding labels labels y_i and not the actual data set we want to predict on. The optimizer $\hat{w}$, which minimizes the objective on the training data set is then used on unseen data in the hope that it generalizes well to unseen data.

Different instantiations of the prediction function f, the loss function l and the regularizer $\Omega(w)$ in the canonical objective outlined above actually yield a broad set of different supervised learning algorithm including logistic regression, Support Vector Machines or LASSO and RIDGE regression as.

Solvers. The most commonly used instantiations of the loss functions l have actually been designed to be both convex and differentiable, which guarantees the existence of a minimizer $\hat{w}$. This enables the application of batch gradient descent (BGD) and similar methods as a solver. BGD iteratively updates the model weights according to the following step using the gradient of the loss until convergence:

$$w' = w - \eta \left(\sum_{(x,y)\in(X,Y)} \frac{\partial}{\partial w} l\left(f_w\left(x\right), y\right) + \lambda \frac{\partial}{\partial w} \Omega\left(w\right) \right)$$

Unfortunately the batch gradient des cent algorithm requires to process the entire training data set to compute just one gradient update. In particular for very large data sets, stochastic gradient descent (SGD) is thus a more popular alternative to BGD. Here. each data point, or a small "mini-batch" of data, is used to compute a gradient update instead of the entire data set:

$$w' = w - \eta \left(\frac{\partial}{\partial w} l \left(f_w \left(x \right), y \right) + \lambda \frac{\partial}{\partial w} \Omega \left(w \right) \right)$$

2.3 Matrix Factorization

Another quite popular and successful category of machine learning algorithms are recommender systems, where the task is to identify and recommend items that a user might like based on historical data of user-item interactions, a technique called collaborative filtering (CF). Due to their success in the Netflix Prize, latent factor models based on matrix factorization [37] are a popular choice for this task. One common approach to compute such recommendations in the context of distributed data processing systems is *Alternating Least Squares (ALS)* [7,55]. The historical data consists of ratings r assembled in a ratings matrix $R = \{r_{i,j}\}$ with the dimensions $n_u \times n_i$ where n_u is the number of users and n_i is the number of items. The goal is to finds a low rank approximation to this matrix based on the product of two, significantly smaller matrices: U and M such that $UM \approx R$, where $U : n_u \times k$ and $M : k \times n_i$ and k is the rank. ALS finds the approximation by solving the following objective:

$$min_{U,M} \sum_{(i,j) \in I} \left(r_{i,j} - u_i^T m_j \right)^2 + \lambda \left(\sum_i n_{u_i} ||u_i||^2 + \sum_j n_{m_j} ||m_j||^2 \right)$$

where I is the set of (user, item) pairs for which ratings exist. Alternating least squares solves this objective by alternatingly holding either U or M fixed and solving a least squared problem to fit the "non-fixed" low-rank matrix. Alternatively, the objective can also be solved with Stochastic Gradient Decent [56] as introduced above. Here we randomly calculate gradient updates for a randomly chosen (u, v) pair. SGD is a fast and popular method to solve a Matrix Factorization problem, however it is inherently sequential.

2.4 Deep Learning

The three aforementioned categories of machine learning algorithms: k-means clustering for unsupervised learning, supervised learning based on a regularized optimization approach and matrix factorization for recommendation mining cover a large part of the machine learning applications in practice [3]. However, next to these rather simple but quite effective methods, that have been proven to excel in particular on very large data sets while being comparatively cheap to train, another class of machine learning algorithm has gained significant attention over the last couple of years: the popularity of training neural networks with several layers (so-called "deep architectures") architectures [29] has risen significantly. Such deep neural network architectures (dubbed "deep learning") have generated stunning results on a variety of machine learning tasks that can roughly be categorized as *cognitive tasks* including visual object recognition, object detection and speech recognition [38].

However these achievements did not come for free. Training state of the art neural network architectures for these tasks requires tremendous computational resources. Since there is little established methodology on who to build such network architectures, one often resorts to intuition, know-how and significant "try 'n error" when developing new models, adding to the overall (computational) cost. In consequence, deep learning approaches are not necessarily the "silver bullet" to be applied to every problem setting at hand. In a lot of application settings, the "traditional" approaches presented above turn out to deliver sufficient prediction quality while requiring substantially less computational resources to train.

The systems used to train deep neural networks also substantially differ from general data processing systems. Since the training of such networks is almost exclusively carried out using backpropagation and mini-batch stochastic gradient descent, the requirements are different than those faced by the general purpose data processing systems discussed in Sect. 1. These were build to address the I/O and network communication bottlenecks generally faced in massively parallel data processing. However, the training of deep neural networks is usually bound by computational resources. Thus, dedicated systems like TensorFlow [4], CNTK [53] or MXNet [20] were built and optimized for the particular use case of training deep neural networks to a degree that was not possible for general purpose distributed data flow systems, as the training algorithm (backpropagation) as well as the data model (tensors) was already consensus and thus fixed.

Another important reason for the recent success of deep neural networks can also be found in the availability of additional computational resources in the form of GPUs, which provide at least an order magnitude more floating point operations per second while being more power and cost-efficient than traditional CPUs. These affordable computational resources being readily available actually enabled the quite computation-intensive training of artificial neural networks with "deep" architectures, which often translates to solving a non-convex optimization problem, within reasonable time-frames. The obvious successes of deep neural networks also prompted the development of purpose-built acceleration hardware, e.g. Tensor Processing Units (TPUs) by Google, to further speed up the training process.

Not least in order to steer the development of such hardware in a sensible way, benchmarks tailored for deep learning settings are evermore important, however given the intricacies of training deep learning models (e.g. degrading generalization performance with increasing batch sizes [33]), and the level of specialization of the systems involved, this can certainly be viewed as a separate problem domain in and of itself and orthogonal to the aspects of benchmarking general purpose data processing systems for machine learning workloads discussed in this work. For example, the recently introduced initiatives DAWNBench [21], an

End-to-End Deep Learning Benchmark Competition that invites submissions of runtimes for specified tasks as well as MLPerf [2] that extends this concept to a more broad set of tasks tackle exactly this issue and are thus orthogonal to the work discussed in this paper.

3 Model Quality

Next to traditional runtime performance, benchmark experiments for machine learning workloads have to take into consideration an important additional dimension: the inherent quality of trained models.

While conventional database queries have a deterministic result set which the database system will always return, no matter which execution plan was chosen by the database optimizer to produce the result, different machine learning approaches produce models with different prediction quality when trained on the exact same data set. Popular empirical evaluations of various supervised learning approaches show this [16,17]. Not only do different machine learning approaches yield models of different quality, they also have different inherent runtime complexity with respect to the number of training data points. When benchmarking data processing systems for machine learning workloads we are thus faced with a trade-off space spawned by the runtime of algorithms and the quality of the models that they produce. Additionally, algorithms may or may not be a suitable fit for the underlying systems paradigm and thus lead to additional inefficiencies when being implemented on top of a distributed data processing sytem. As we mentioned in Sect. 1, the algorithms chosen for evaluation experiments in the corresponding systems papers were mostly learning algorithms those that are well suited for the underlying system paradigm rather than state of the art methods. In consequence, it is imperative to take into account the dimension of model quality when benchmarking data processing systems for machine learning workloads and to conceive experiments that explore the trade-off space spawned by the runtime of machine learning algorithms and the quality of the models that they produce. Additional, state of the art, single node machine learning algorithms, that may not be a good fit of a distributed data processing systems paradigm, should be leveraged as competitive baselines for these experiments.

3.1 Experiments and Workloads

To address the requirements and explore the trade-off space spawned by the runtime of machine learning algorithms and the quality of the models that they produce, we propose to run training experiments with and without evaluation of model quality on a held-out test data sets for varying amounts of iterations. This way we can obtain both: the runtime of training itself and the corresponding model quality at different points during training. (As distributed data processing systems such as *Apache Spark* do not allow intermediate evaluation of models, this translates to re-running the training with different numbers of iterations from scratch, measuring the training time and subsequently evaluating model quality on a held out set of test data.)

Parameter Tuning. Machine learning algorithms tend to come with tunable parameters specific to each model. The search for the optimal values for such so-called hyperparameters can have significant impact on the resulting model quality. To provide a level playing field, we designated equal time slots for parameter tuning with the means provided by the libraries evaluated across all systems and libraries. A setting which reflects the reality in which practitioners also only have limited amounts of time available for tuning parameters [10].

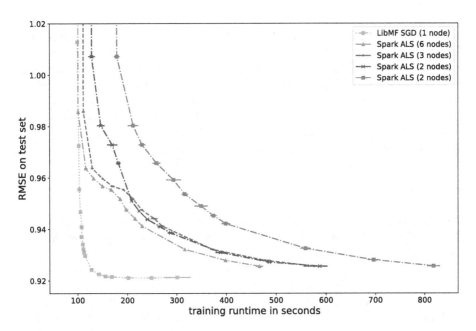

Fig. 1. Matrix factorization of the Netflix prize data set using Apache *Spark MLlib's* ALS implementation on six *big* (24 cores, 256 GB Ram) cluster nodes and *LibMF* one *big* node. The plots show the root mean squared error (RMSE) achieved on a test set achieved after a certain amount of training time. The Spark implementation takes significantly more time to converge in comparison to the single machine library LibMF, even when executed on multiple nodes.

Experiment 1: Matrix Factorization: We propose to run matrix factorization for collaborative filtering as introduced in Sect. 2. While the presented Alternating Least Squares approach is implemented in all popular distributed data processing systems, single machine libraries using parallel SGD such as *LibMF*[1] [56] can be used for the single machine experiments. Next to training runtime, we suggest to measure the Root Mean Squared Error (RMSE) as a metric for model quality. Figure 1 shows the results of such an experiment comparing *Spark MLLib's* ALS implementation against *LibMF*. It becomes apparent that such an

---

[1] https://www.csie.ntu.edu.tw/~cjlin/libmf/.

experiment shows the overhead one incurs for running a machine learning algorithm on a scalable systems such as Apache Spark. The Spark implementation takes significantly more time to converge in comparison to the single machine library LibMF, even when executed on multiple nodes. The experiments were executed on nodes with: We thus propose experiments to explore all of these dimensions.2 x AMD Opteron 6238 CPU with 12 Cores @ 2.6 GHz (24 cores), 256 GB RAM, 8x 2 TB Disk, 6 × GE Ethernet via a Cisco C2969-48TD-L Rack Switch.

Experiment 2: Supervised Learning: We propose to evaluate logistic regression and gradient boosted trees in both distributed data processing systems and with sophisticated single machine libraries such as *Vowpal Wabbit*[2] (LR SGD), *XGBoost*[3], *LightGBM*[4] or *CatBoost*[5]. Next to training runtime, we suggest to use the Area Under the Curve (AuC) metric, as it is not sensitive to skew in the test data set. As data set we suggest to use (potentially a subsample) of the Criteo Click Log Data set presented in Sect. 4.3. (In [8] we presented results for this experiment for Apache Spark MLLib.)

4 Scalability

The main premise of big data analytics systems is to scale out computation across many machines in order to speed up I/O and to lower execution time. In light of the massive data set sizes with billions of data points, this necessitates scalable algorithms with respect to the input data size which has at worst linear runtime complexity. With such scalable algorithms, the distributed data processing systems can be leveraged and workloads can be scaled out by merely adding machines in proportion to growing data set sizes. In light of cloud computing, this can be automated and flexibly adjusted via auto-scaling according to the load.

When training machine learning models on such systems, it is thus necessary to utilize algorithms that fulfill the scalability requirement. As an example, consider the common problem faced by web applications that display online advertisement to their users: *click-through rate prediction*. The task is to predict whether a user will click on a displayed ad. Given the massive user bases of popular online web applications, these models are trained on data sets hundreds of terrabytes in size, containing hundreds of billions of data points. This data also tends to be quite sparse (only 10–100 non-zero features per data point) but also very high dimensional (up to 100 billion unique features according to a google tech talk [15]). According to relevant literature, machine learning methods like regularized logistic regression are a popular and effective choice

---

[2] https://github.com/JohnLangford/vowpal_wabbit/.
[3] https://github.com/dmlc/xgboost.
[4] https://github.com/Microsoft/LightGBM.
[5] https://github.com/catboost/catboost.

for the click-through rate prediction problem [18,32,40,44] and a popular choice by practitioners for general supervised learning settings [3] with very large data sets [36].

As we argued in [9], the context of benchmarking data processing systems for scalable machine learning workloads, there are several dimensions of scalability that have to be taken into account:

1. **Scaling the Data:** as the term *big data* suggests, scaling machine learning algorithms to extremely large data set sizes is the most obvious notion of scalability. It is of particular importance to machine learning applications, as it has been shown that even quite simple machine learning models can outperform more complex approaches when trained on sufficiently large data sets [11,31]. This notion of scalability is arguably what the distributed data processing systems introduced in Sect. 1 have been designed and built for.
2. **Scaling the Model Size:** as we indicated above, generalized linear models, which are a popular choice in light of very large amounts of available training data, tend to exhibit very high dimensionality. For example, classification algorithms built on textual data using *n-grams* of words can easily contain 100 million dimensions or more. Models for click-through rate prediction for online advertisements can even reach up to 100 billion dimensions [15]. Thus it is also crucial to examine how distributed data processing systems scale with increasing model dimensionality.

4.1 Experiments and Workloads

In this section we outline the experiments proposed to address the scalability dimensions discussed above. As the hardware setup for on-premise clusters is generally fixed in the short term, we introduce two new experiments to adequately capture the desired scaling dimensions *data* and *model* for this setting and finally complete the scalability experiments by adding the two traditional notions of scaling as experiments - strong scaling and weak scaling:

Experiment 3: Production Scaling: We measure the runtime for training a model of fixed dimensionality varying the size of the training data set on a fixed number of nodes.

Experiment 4: Model Dimensionality Scaling: We measure the runtime for training a model of varying dimensionality on a fixed number of nodes and with constant training data set size. We propose a way to control the dimensionality in Sect. 4.3.

Experiment 5: Strong Scaling: We measure the runtime for training a model on varying amounts of nodes while holding the data set size and model dimensionality fixed.

Experiment 6: Weak Scaling: We measure the runtime for training a model on varying amounts of nodes while also varying the data set size accordingly, such that the problem size per processor as well as the dimensionality of the model remains constant.

4.2   Workloads

We propose to evaluate the following workloads for the scalability experiments outlined above:

- **Regularized Logistic Regression:** run logistic regression with a gradient decent solver as suggested in [9] using the Criteo Click Log data with sub- and super-sampling for scaling the data set size and feature hashing for dimensionality scaling as discussed below in Sect. 4.3.
- **Alternating Least Squares Matrix Factorization:** run ALS on generated data either based on characteristics of existing ratings data sets (e.g. Netflix or MovieLens) as suggested in [49]. For the dimensionality scaling we suggest to vary latent factor dimensionality (the rank) of the two factor matrices.
- **K-Means Clustering:** run the clustering algorithm on generated data discussed below in Sect. 4.3.

4.3   Data Sets

We suggest to rely on generated data for the scalability *unsupervised learning* as well as the *matrix factorization* experiments. (E.g. 100 dimensional data from k Gaussian distributions and add uniform random noise to the data, similar to the data generation for k-means in Mahout [1] and *HiBench* [34].)

For the classification workloads, we suggest the use of the *Criteo Click Logs*[6] data set. This dataset contains click feedback for millions of display ads drawn from a portion of Criteo's traffic over a period of 24 days. It was originally released as part of a Kaggle challenge for click through rate (CTR) prediction. The dataset contains a label indicating the user action as well as 13 numeric and 26 categorical features. The entire data set spawns about 4 billion data points, has a size of 1.5 TB.

As a pre-processing step we propose to use the popular hashing trick [52] to expand the categorical features in the criteo click log data set. This hashing trick transforms the categorical variables by applying a hash function to the feature values and using the hash values as indices of the final feature vector. This is a standard approach when working with the CTR data set from criteo. It also has the nice property that it allows to control the dimensionality of the training data vectors and thus the dimensionality of the supervised machine learning model to be trained. This can be applied in the model scaling experiment we proposed as *Experiment 4* above.

---

[6] http://labs.criteo.com/downloads/download-terabyte-click-logs/.

5   Related Work

Benchmarking and performance analysis of data distributed data processing and analytics frameworks have received some attention in the research community [43,47,50,51]. However most of the research papers focus on evaluating the runtime and execution speed of non-representative workloads with respect to machine learning such as *WordCount, Grep* or *Sort*. The ones that do focus on machine learning workloads [9,14] neglect quality metrics such as accuracy or AuC completely in their experimental evaluations. Unfortunately, the actual systems papers of the data processing systems and paradigms such as Apache Spark, Apache Flink or Graphlab [5,41,54] themselves do not contain any experiments that would provide insight into the obtained machine learning model quality. The *MLlib* paper introducing the Machine Learning library of Apache Spark for example only reports speed-up of the runtime relative to an older version of MLlib itself.

On the other hand there exist several efforts in evaluating a broad spectrum of popular machine learning algorithms empirically [16,17] with a focus on prediction quality. However the authors neglect the runtime of the algorithm and do not consider distributed data processing systems.

Finally, there has been work comparing the runtime of popular graph processing algorithms for distributed data processing systems against a competent implementation on a single machine [45]. The authors propose *COST (the Configuration that Outperforms a Single Thread)* as a new metric for distributed data processing systems. The work showed that for the simple graph processing algorithms evaluated, none of distributed data processing systems considered managed to outperform a competent single-threaded implementation using a high-end 2014 laptop. In contrast to the work presented here, the authors only consider graph algorithms with a fixed result set and thus do not address issue of model prediction quality and base their findings solely on runtimes published in other papers, not their own experiments.

6   Conclusion

Distributed data processing systems that have originally been conceived to scale out data-intensive computations on very large data sets to many nodes have become popular choices to scale out the execution of machine learning algorithms as well. However, there is still a lack of benchmarks to adequately assess the performance of scaling out machine learning workloads on such data processing systems, consisting of an objective set of workloads, experiments and metrics.

In this paper, we presented work on such a benchmark of distributed data processing systems for machine learning workloads. In Sect. 3 we argued that there is an additional challenge being faced when evaluating machine learning algorithms the dimension of model quality. We proposed experiments to explore the trade-off space spawned by the runtime of algorithms and the quality of the models that they produce. We also made the case that state of the art single machine libraries should serve as sophisticated baselines in such experiments. Our empirical evaluation of Apache Spark MLLibs alternating least squares algorithm and LibMF as an SGD based single machine library for matrix factorization on the netflix prize data set indicates that latest generation distributed data processing systems like Apache Spark do incur a non-negligible overhead and thus require more hardware resources to obtain comparable prediction quality with a competent single machine implementation within a comparable time-frame. Additionally in Sect. 4 we discussed several dimensions of scalability in the context of distributed data processing systems. We proposed experiments that cover both: scalability with respect to the input data set size as well as the model dimensionality. With this we specified what we deem to be a core set of experiments that constitute a benchmark for distributed data processing systems for scalable machine learning workloads.

Acknowledgments. This work has been supported by the German Ministry for Education and Research as Berlin Big Data Center BBDC (funding mark 01IS14013A).

References

1. https://mahout.apache.org/
2. https://mlperf.org/
3. https://www.kaggle.com/surveys/2017
4. Abadi, M., et al.: TensorFlow: a system for large-scale machine learning. In: OSDI, pp. 265–283. USENIX Association (2016)
5. Alexandrov, A., et al.: The stratosphere platform for big data analytics. VLDB J. **23**(6), 939–964 (2014)
6. Baru, C., et al.: Discussion of BigBench: a proposed industry standard performance benchmark for big data. In: Nambiar, R., Poess, M. (eds.) TPCTC 2014. LNCS, vol. 8904, pp. 44–63. Springer, Cham (2015). https://doi.org/10.1007/978-3-319-15350-6_4
7. Bell, R.M., Koren, Y.: Scalable collaborative filtering with jointly derived neighborhood interpolation weights. In: Seventh IEEE International Conference on Data Mining (ICDM 2007), pp. 43–52, October 2007
8. Boden, C., Rabl, T., Markl, V.: Distributed machine learning-but at what cost?
9. Boden, C., Spina, A., Rabl, T., Markl, V.: Benchmarking data flow systems for scalable machine learning. In: Proceedings of the 4th Algorithms and Systems on MapReduce and Beyond, BeyondMR 2017, pp. 5:1–5:10. ACM, New York (2017)
10. Böse, J.-H., et al.: Probabilistic demand forecasting at scale. Proc. VLDB Endow. **10**(12), 1694–1705 (2017)
11. Brants, T., Popat, A.C., Xu, P., Och, F.J., Dean, J.: Large language models in machine translation. In: EMNLP, pp. 858–867 (2007)
12. Brin, S., Page, L.: The anatomy of a large-scale hypertextual Web search engine. Comput. Netw. ISDN Syst. **30**(1), 107–117 (1998). Proceedings of the Seventh International World Wide Web Conference
13. Bu, Y., Howe, B., Balazinska, M., Ernst, M.D.: Haloop: efficient iterative data processing on large clusters. Proc. VLDB Endow. **3**(1–2), 285–296 (2010)

14. Cai, Z., Gao, Z.J., Luo, S., Perez, L.L., Vagena, Z., Jermaine, C.: A comparison of platforms for implementing and running very large scale machine learning algorithms. In: Proceedings of the 2014 ACM SIGMOD International Conference on Management of Data, SIGMOD 2014, pp. 1371–1382 (2014)
15. Caninil, K.: Sibyl: a system for large scale supervised machine learning (2012)
16. Caruana, R., Karampatziakis, N., Yessenalina, A.: An empirical evaluation of supervised learning in high dimensions. In: Proceedings of the 25th International Conference on Machine Learning, ICML 2008, pp. 96–103. ACM, New York (2008)
17. Caruana, R., Niculescu-Mizil, A.: An empirical comparison of supervised learning algorithms. In: Proceedings of the 23rd International Conference on Machine Learning, ICML 2006, pp. 161–168. ACM, New York (2006)
18. Chapelle, O., Manavoglu, E., Rosales, R.: Simple and scalable response prediction for display advertising. ACM Trans. Intell. Syst. Technol. 5(4), 61:1–61:34 (2014)
19. Chen, T., Guestrin, C.: XGBoost: a scalable tree boosting system. In: Proceedings of the 22nd ACM SIGKDD International Conference on Knowledge Discovery and Data Mining, KDD 2016, pp. 785–794. ACM, New York (2016)
20. Chen, T., et al.: MXNet: a flexible and efficient machine learning library for heterogeneous distributed systems. CoRR, abs/1512.01274 (2015)
21. Coleman, C., et al.: DAWNBench: an end-to-end deep learning benchmark and competition. In: ML Systems Workshop @ NIPS 2017, vol. 100, no. 101, p. 102 (2017)
22. Das, A.S., Datar, M., Garg, A., Rajaram, S.: Google news personalization: scalable online collaborative filtering. In: Proceedings of the 16th International Conference on World Wide Web, WWW 2007, pp. 271–280. ACM, New York (2007)
23. Dean, J., Ghemawat, S.: MapReduce: simplified data processing on large clusters. Commun. ACM 51(1), 107–113 (2008)
24. Domingos, P.: A few useful things to know about machine learning. Commun. ACM 55(10), 78–87 (2012)
25. Ekanayake, J., et al.: Twister: a runtime for iterative MapReduce. In: Proceedings of the 19th ACM International Symposium on High Performance Distributed Computing, HPDC 2010, pp. 810–818. ACM, New York (2010)
26. Ewen, S., Tzoumas, K., Kaufmann, M., Markl, V.: Spinning fast iterative data flows. Proc. VLDB Endow. 5, 1268–1279 (2012)
27. Friedman, J.H.: Greedy function approximation: a gradient boosting machine. Ann. Stat. 29, 1189–1232 (2000)
28. Ghazal, A., et al.: Bigbench: towards an industry standard benchmark for big data analytics. In: Proceedings of the 2013 ACM SIGMOD International Conference on Management of Data, SIGMOD 2013, pp. 1197–1208. ACM, New York (2013)
29. Goodfellow, I., Bengio, Y., Courville, A.: Deep Learning. The MIT Press, Cambridge (2016)
30. Gustafson, J.L.: Reevaluating Amdahl's law. Commun. ACM 31(5), 532–533 (1988)
31. Halevy, A., Norvig, P., Pereira, F.: The unreasonable effectiveness of data. IEEE Intell. Syst. 24(2), 8–12 (2009)
32. He, X., et al.: Practical lessons from predicting clicks on ads at Facebook. In: Proceedings of the Eighth International Workshop on Data Mining for Online Advertising, ADKDD 2014, pp. 5:1–5:9. ACM, New York (2014)
33. Hoffer, E., Hubara, I., Soudry, D.: Train longer, generalize better: closing the generalization gap in large batch training of neural networks. In: NIPS, pp. 1729–1739 (2017)

34. Huang, S., Huang, J., Dai, J., Xie, T., Huang, B.: The HiBench benchmark suite: characterization of the MapReduce-based data analysis. In: Agrawal, D., Candan, K.S., Li, W.-S. (eds.) New Frontiers in Information and Software as Services. LNBIP, vol. 74, pp. 209–228. Springer, Heidelberg (2011). https://doi.org/10.1007/978-3-642-19294-4_9
35. Jagadish, H.V., et al.: Big data and its technical challenges. Commun. ACM **57**(7), 86–94 (2014)
36. Jimmy, L., Kolcz, A.: Large-scale machine learning at Twitter. In: SIGMOD 2012 (2012)
37. Koren, Y., Bell, R., Volinsky, C.: Matrix factorization techniques for recommender systems. Computer **42**(8), 30–37 (2009)
38. LeCun, Y., Bengio, Y., Hinton, G.: Deep learning. Nature **521**(7553), 436 (2015)
39. Lin, J., Dyer, C.: Data-Intensive Text Processing with MapReduce. Morgan and Claypool Publishers, San Rafael (2010)
40. Ling, X., Deng, W., Gu, C., Zhou, H., Li, C., Sun, F.: Model ensemble for click prediction in Bing search ads. In: Proceedings of the 26th International Conference on World Wide Web Companion, WWW 2017 Companion, pp. 689–698, Republic and Canton of Geneva, Switzerland. International World Wide Web Conferences Steering Committee (2017)
41. Low, Y., Bickson, D., Gonzalez, J., Guestrin, C., Kyrola, A., Hellerstein, J.M.: Distributed GraphLab: a framework for machine learning and data mining in the cloud. Proce. VLDB Endow. **5**(8), 716–727 (2012)
42. Low, Y., Gonzalez, J.E., Kyrola, A., Bickson, D., Guestrin, C.E., Hellerstein, J.: GraphLab: a new framework for parallel machine learning. arXiv preprint arXiv:1408.2041 (2014)
43. Marcu, O.C., Costan, A., Antoniu, G., Pérez-Henéndez, M.S.: Spark versus flink: understanding performance in big data analytics frameworks. IEEE CLUSTER **2016**, 433–442 (2016)
44. McMahan, H.B., et al.: Ad click prediction: a view from the trenches. In: KDD 2013. ACM (2013)
45. McSherry, F., Isard, M., Murray, D.G.: Scalability! But at what cost? In: USENIX HOTOS 2015. USENIX Association (2015)
46. Meng, X., et al.: MLlib: machine learning in Apache spark. J. Mach. Learn. Res. **17**(1), 1235–1241 (2016)
47. Ousterhout, K., Rasti, R., Ratnasamy, S., Shenker, S., Chun, B.-G.: Making sense of performance in data analytics frameworks. In: Proceedings of the 12th USENIX Conference on Networked Systems Design and Implementation, NSDI 2015, pp. 293–307. USENIX Association, Berkeley (2015)
48. Richardson, M., Dominowska, E., Ragno, R.: Predicting clicks: estimating the click-through rate for new ads. In: WWW 2007. ACM (2007)
49. Schelter, S., Boden, C., Schenck, M., Alexandrov, A., Markl, V.: Distributed matrix factorization with MapReduce using a series of broadcast-joins. In: ACM RecSys 2013 (2013)
50. Shi, J., et al.: Clash of the Titans: MapReduce vs. spark for large scale data analytics. Proc. VLDB Endow. **8**(13), 2110–2121 (2015)
51. Veiga, J., Expósito, R.R., Pardo, X.C., Taboada, G.L., Tourifio, J.: Performance evaluation of big data frameworks for large-scale data analytics. IEEE BigData **2016**, 424–431 (2016)

52. Weinberger, K., Dasgupta, A., Langford, J., Smola, A., Attenberg, J.: Feature hashing for large scale multitask learning. In: Proceedings of the 26th Annual International Conference on Machine Learning, ICML 2009, pp. 1113–1120. ACM, New York (2009)
53. Yu, D., et al.: An introduction to computational networks and the computational network toolkit. Microsoft Technical report MSR-TR-2014-112 (2014)
54. Zaharia, M., et al.: Resilient distributed datasets: a fault-tolerant abstraction for in-memory cluster computing. In: NSDI 2012 (2012)
55. Zhou, Y., Wilkinson, D., Schreiber, R., Pan, R.: Large-scale parallel collaborative filtering for the Netflix prize. In: Fleischer, R., Xu, J. (eds.) AAIM 2008. LNCS, vol. 5034, pp. 337–348. Springer, Heidelberg (2008). https://doi.org/10.1007/978-3-540-68880-8_32
56. Zhuang, Y., Chin, W.-S., Juan, Y.-C., Lin, C.-J.: A fast parallel SGD for matrix factorization in shared memory systems. In: Proceedings of the 7th ACM Conference on Recommender Systems, RecSys 2013, pp. 249–256. ACM, New York (2013)

Characterizing the Performance and Resilience of HCI Clusters with the TPCx-HCI Benchmark

H. Reza Taheri[1(✉)], Gary Little[2], Bhavik Desai[2], Andrew Bond[3],
Doug Johnson[4], and Greg Kopczynski[1]

[1] VMware, Inc., Palo Alto, USA
{rtaheri,gregw}@vmware.com
[2] Nutanix, Inc., San Jose, USA
{gary,bhavik.desai}@nutanix.com
[3] Red Hat, Inc., Raleigh, USA
abond@redhat.com
[4] InfoSizing, Inc., Manitou Springs, USA
doug@sizing.com

Abstract. We use the newly-released TPCx-HCI benchmark to characterize the performance and resilience properties of Hyper-Converged Infrastructure clusters. We demonstrate that good performance on an HCI cluster requires delivering all properties of high IOPS, low latencies, low CPU overhead, and uniform access to data from all Nodes. We show that unless the cluster can quickly and efficiently rebalance the VMs after a change in the workload, performance will be severely impacted.

We use the data accessibility test of TPCx-HCI to show how performance is impacted by rebuilding traffic after a Node goes down, and how long it takes for the rebuilding to finish.

Keywords: Performance benchmarking · Hyper-converged infrastructure performance · Industry-standard benchmarks

1 Introduction

1.1 The Need for TPCx-HCI

Hyper-Converged Infrastructure (HCI) is a term used to describe a combination of hardware and software which are pooled together to form a cluster capable of running virtual machines. Each Node runs a hypervisor on which the user virtual machines, e.g. databases and clients, execute. Nodes within an HCI cluster cooperate to form a filesystem which is accessible across the cluster. A shared filesystem is critical for virtualized environments because it is expected that a virtual machine can migrate from one Node to another without making a disk-copy.

There are many TPC benchmarks that can be used to measure against a single machine with a single address space. The TPCx-V benchmark [4] was the first to support aggregation of multiple independent database instances to create a single

© Springer Nature Switzerland AG 2019
R. Nambiar and M. Poess (Eds.): TPCTC 2018, LNCS 11135, pp. 58–70, 2019.
https://doi.org/10.1007/978-3-030-11404-6_5

benchmark metric. TPCx-HCI extends the ideas of TPCx-V to measure the aggregation of multiple Nodes in a cluster as well as multiple databases per Node.

Accordingly, the purpose of this benchmark is to measure the ability of the hardware and software to work together to provide a computing resource which is scalable and tolerant of failures. With TPCx-HCI, the database engine remains constant across all submissions, so effectively, TPCx-HCI measures the following components

- *Hardware* – CPU, Memory, Storage and Network performance
- *Hypervisor* - Overhead of virtualization, the ability for the hypervisor to handle consolidation and multi-tenancy
- *Storage* - Storage overhead, response times and resiliency, multi-tenancy
- *Network* - Provides the underlying capabilities of the storage and hypervisor (VM migration & storage replication).

TPCx-HCI attempts to measure the above components for the following attributes:

- Speed - How much work can be achieved per unit of time
- Stability - How resilient is the cluster to component failures
- Scale - Given a cluster at steady state, what fraction of the additional capacity can be consumed without intervention.

To our knowledge, no existing benchmarks measure these three dimensions in a cohesive fashion

1.2   History of the Benchmark

The TPCx-HCI benchmark owes its origins to the TPCx-V benchmark. TPCx-V was introduced in an earlier TPCTC Workshop [4], as well as subsequent papers detailing the architecture [1] and tuning procedures [2] for the benchmark. TPCx-V was formally accepted as a benchmark standard by the TPC in November 2015 [6].

In early 2017, the TPC subcommittee set out to extend the TPCx-V Specification and Benchmark Kit to Hyper-Converged Infrastructure clusters. A TPCx-HCI Specification was approved in December 2017. A quick development cycle was possible since extending TPCx-V from a single server to a cluster of servers was a natural next step.

1.3   Hyper-Converged Infrastructure

Let us use the following quote from the TPCx-HCI Benchmark Specification to describe the kind of systems this benchmark targets (a VMMS refers to a Virtual Machine Management Software, commonly known as a Hypervisor)

> A **TPCx-HCI Cluster** consists of at least 2 **Nodes**, each running a single instance of the **VMMS**. The HCI software provides one or more storage abstractions that are distributed across the **Nodes** and uniformly accessible from all the **Nodes** in the **Cluster**, such that any running database can be migrated "live" to any host without a "Data Copy". In other word, it is expected that all the nodes in a **TPCx-HCI Cluster** present what is commonly known as "Shared Storage".

*All physical storage must be locally attached to the individual **Nodes**, and no external SAN (Storage Area Network) or NAS (Network Attached Storage) nor any other physical means of providing external shared storage among the **Nodes** of the **Cluster** may be used in the **SUT**. Regardless of the number of **Nodes** (n) in a **TPCx-HCI Cluster**, every storage abstraction must provide redundancy to meet the **TPCx-HCI Data Accessibility** test. A **TPCx-HCI Cluster** of n **Nodes** must be capable of demonstrating uninterrupted **Data Accessibility** of all storage abstractions and **Durability** of all committed transactions on (n-1) **Nodes** in the event of unmanaged loss of power to any single **Node**.*

2 Architecture of TPCx-HCI

2.1 Overview

The System Under Test (SUT) is divided into multiple Tiles. **Tile** is the unit of replication of TPCx-HCI configuration and load distribution. Each Tile consists of 4 Groups, and all Tiles contribute identical proportions to the total load of the SUT. Over the full measurement interval, each of the four Groups contributes an *average* of 10%, 20%, 30%, and 40% of the total throughput of the Tile, respectively.

Each Group consists of one Tier A Virtual Machine and two transaction-specific Tier B Virtual Machines, for a total of 12 VMs in each Tile. VM1 of each Group contains that Group's Tier A, which runs the business logic application, and has the frames code functions (DML) that issue the database transactions. VM1 does not contain a database. VM2 is the Tier B VM that holds the DSS database and accepts the two storage load-heavy DSS transactions. VM3 is the Tier B VM that holds the OLTP database and accepts the 9 CPU load-heavy OLTP transactions.

2.2 Benchmark Kit

As noted above, the TPCx-HCI benchmark is a very modest derivative of the TPCx-V benchmark. In fact, modification of the TPCx-V benchmark kit to support TPCx-HCI mostly involved modifying the reporter code to print a report for either type of benchmark. It would be fair to say that the TPCx-HCI benchmark runs the TPCx-V benchmark, but in a hyperconverged infrastructure configuration.

As such, the five software components of the TPCx-HCI benchmark driver are the same as those for the TPCx-V benchmark; four that are used to drive the workload and one to provide reporting functionality:

- **Prime client:** The prime client (vdriver.jar) is the benchmark execution controller. It coordinates and controls the behavior of the Customer Emulator (CE) client(s), Market Exchange Emulator (MEE) clients(s) and Tier A SUT connectors through RMI connections to each.
- **CE client:** The client emulator (vce.jar) is responsible for emulating customers, requesting a service of the brokerage house, providing the necessary input for the requested service, etc.

- **MEE client:** The market exchange emulator (vmee.jar) is responsible for emulating the stock exchanges by providing services to the brokerage house, per-forming requested trades, providing market activity updates, etc.
- **Tier A SUT connector:** The Tier A SUT connector (vconnector.jar) receives the transaction requests from the CE and MEE clients and sends queries to its Tier B databases.
- **Reporter:** The reporter (reporter.jar) performs the self-validation checks against the transaction log data and (optionally) creates an executive summary report.

Except for the reporter that is run independently, the relationship between the other four software components are represented, below (Fig. 1):

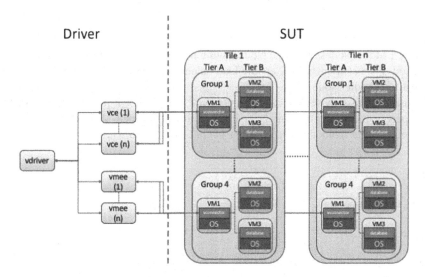

Fig. 1. Components of the TPCx-HCI benchmark

Note that the actual interaction between these components is more complex than this illustration suggests. For example, while all communication between the Prime client and the other three components are RMI connections for benchmark coordination and control, the other three components also use separate connections on which they execute transactions between the driver and the SUT.

2.3   TPCx-HCI Express Kit

TPCx-HCI is a TPC *Express* benchmark, meaning that a kit is provided, and the test sponsor is required to run the kit as is. The kit has code to create and populate the databases, run the benchmark, self-validate and self-audit the results, and produce the Executive Summary for the Full Disclosure Report. The test sponsor does not need, nor is allowed, to write any code for the benchmark. With its self-validation and self-auditing features, the audit process for the benchmark should be a lot lighter than previous Enterprise TPC benchmarks.

3   Characteristics of the Benchmark

3.1   Elasticity Feature

One of the defining characteristics of HCI systems is uniform access to data from all Nodes (see Sects. 1.1 and 1.3). To evaluate how well an HCI cluster delivers that property, the TPCx-HCI workload was designed in a way that achieving good performance would benefit from migration of VMs among the nodes in the cluster. Aside from evaluating the uniformity of access to data, this measures the live migration speed, another important property of HCI clusters.

In keeping with the tradition of TPC benchmarks, the TPCx-HCI Specification does not *require* live migrations, nor does it choreograph how, when, or where the VMs should be migrated. Instead, the benchmark relies on the following two requirements:

1. At the beginning of the benchmark run on an N-Node cluster, all the VMs should be on N-1 of the Nodes, with one Node having no VMs. Midway through the warm-up period, the test sponsor may enable load balancing on the cluster, allowing VMs to float to the idle Node
2. Using the elasticity feature in the benchmark (see [3] for a full description of this property), the proportion of the overall load sent to each VM is changed every 12 min, while maintaining a constant overall load as shown in Fig. 2.

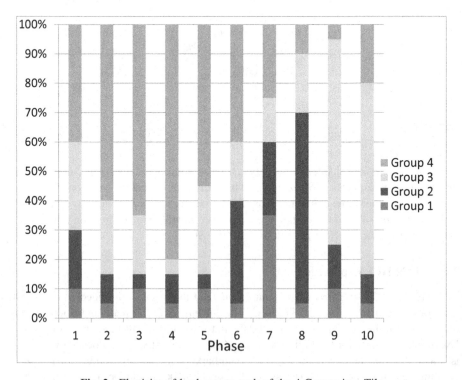

Fig. 2. Elasticity of load sent to each of the 4 Groups in a Tile

The benchmark specification does not require that VMs be migrated after the initial warm-up, or at any subsequent time. It is up to the test sponsor to use a load-balancing feature if it is available. If not, we can still have a valid benchmark run, but a run that leaves one Node unused, losing potential performance.

3.2   Tile Count

Using a Tile based architecture is common in virtualization benchmarks [5, 6], where every Tile handles the same amount of load. A TPCx-HCI *Tile* consists of 4 *Groups* [1], each with 3 VMs. The elasticity feature of the benchmark varies what percentage of a Tile's load is directed to each Group, while maintaining a constant load level for the whole Tile.

So, if it were possible to place a Tile in its entirety on one Node, the *overall* load on that Node would not change during the benchmark run, even if the *distribution of that load among the VMs* in the Tile changes.

To encourage the use of a load balancer, and reward the vendor whose load balancing product is fast and efficient, the specification requires a Tile count [3] that is not an integral product of the node count. This makes it impossible to trivially achieve balanced performance by statically assigning each Tile to a separate node.

4   Analysis

In this section, we will focus on how well TPCx-HCI can evaluate the efficiency of the cluster load balancer, as well as testing that access to data is uniform among all the Nodes. Of course, the benchmark also evaluates many other properties of the System Under Test: processor hardware, underlying storage, networking, hypervisor, etc. Testing of those properties has been covered in previous publications [1–4] regarding the TPCx-V benchmark, which was the starting point for TPCx-HCI.

4.1   Configuration of the System Under Test

Tests in Sect. 4 were run on a

- 4-node cluster of Dell R730xd servers:
  - two-socket, Broadwell processors
  - 8 1.8 TB SSD capacity drives and 2 NVMe cache devices.
  - 512 GB of memory.

  VMware vSphere 6.5 with vSAN 6.6.1.

4.2   Performance of 4 Tiles on 4 Nodes

To see the value of the load balancing and of the uniformity of access, we use the case of 4 Tiles on 4 Nodes as the baseline. Although this is a non-compliant TPCx-HCI configuration (see Sect. 3.2), it establishes the performance of an ideally balanced environment.

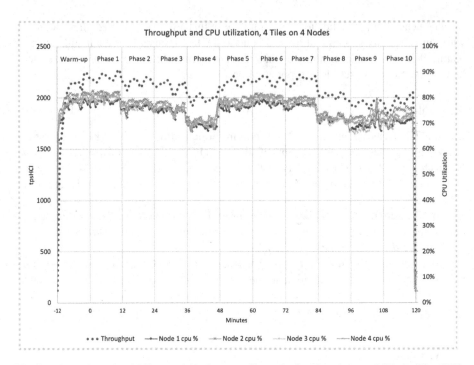

Fig. 3. Throughput for 4 Tiles on 4 Nodes, one tile statically placed on each Node. The CPU utilization curves of all 4 Nodes are very similar, and track the throughput curve

In Fig. 3, it is hard to tell apart the throughput curve and the 4 CPU utilization curves. But this is exactly the point: the 4 Nodes are nicely balanced, and the utilizations track the throughput curve, which is relatively flat despite the variation in load to each VM. The fluctuations in throughput are mostly due to PostgreSQL checkpoints, which occur every 6 min: There are two dips in throughput in each 12-minute Phase.

4.3 Performance of 5 Tiles on 3 Nodes Without Rebalancing

A valid TPCx-HCI run on 4 Nodes requires *starting* with 5 Tiles (or perhaps 9, 13, etc. depending on performance) spread over 3 Nodes. Rebalancing is not required.

Figure 4 shows that performance suffers badly when 5 Tiles are placed on 3 Nodes. When the phase-to-phase elasticity changes the load that is directed to different Groups, the distribution of load among Nodes is no longer balanced, resulting in deep drops in performance, and Nodes whose utilizations no longer match. Node 1 has a very low utilization. There are no VMs on that Node, but the Node still runs the HCI software, and sees a 10% CPU utilization.

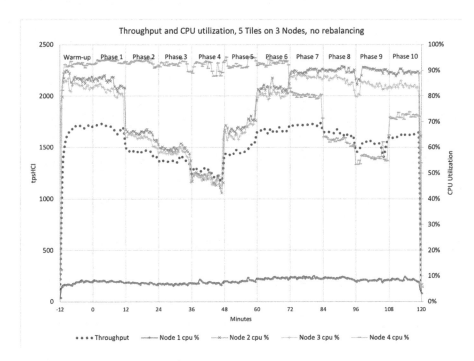

Fig. 4. Throughput and CPU utilizations for 5 Tiles on 3 Nodes

4.4 Performance of 5 Tiles on 4 Nodes with Rebalancing

Figure 5 shows a typical TPCx-HCI run. The 60 VMs of 5 Tiles are placed on Nodes 2-4. We increased the warm-up period to 24 min to better demonstrate the rebalancing behavior. As per TPCx-HCI specification, at the midway point of the warm-up period (minute 12), rebalancing was enabled. The vSphere Distributed Resource Scheduler (DRS) [8] rebalanced the load by moving some VMs to Node 1. The load remains constant until the end of Phase 1. At this point, the load levels of all 60 VMs change, some drastically. The load on the 4 Nodes is not balanced, and DRS has to move some VMs around to balance the load. The rebalancing occurs automatically, there is no manual intervention. The DRS algorithm chooses which VMs to migrate.

Figure 6 shows that 7 migrations are necessary at the very beginning when Node 1 is idle. It is interesting to note that after the initial rebalancing, migrating only 0–5 VMs is enough to rebalance the cluster.

Although it might appear that the throughput fluctuates too much in this run, the fluctuations are well within the limits specified by the benchmark. The *Sustainable Performance* requirements are that "The aggregate throughput computed over any period of one hour, sliding over the **Steady State** by increments of twelve minutes, varies from the **Reported Throughput** by no more than 2%", and "computed over any period of twelve minutes, sliding over the **Steady State** by increments of one minute, varies from the **Reported Throughput** by no more than 20%". These two metrics for this run were 1.267% and 10.297%, respectively.

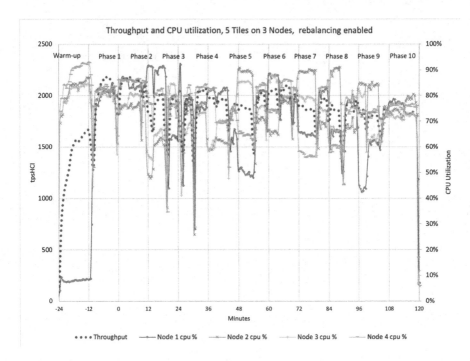

Fig. 5. Throughput and CPU utilizations with 5 Tiles on 4 Nodes. The run started with VMs on Nodes 2–4. Rebalancing started at minute 12.

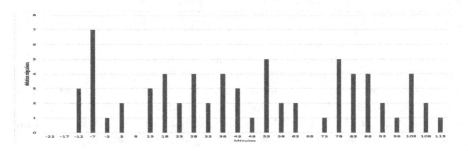

Fig. 6. vMotion migrations to rebalance the cluster

The overall throughput of the *compliant, load-balancing* run in Fig. 5 was 1,898.89 tpsHCI; compared to 2,087.26 tpsHCI for the *baseline, non-compliant* run in Fig. 3 for a ratio of 91%. Not all of the 9% drop was due to the Nodes running unbalanced (for short intervals). We conducted an experiment similar to the compliant, load-balancing run in Fig. 5, but with 4 Tiles, and observed 1,980.43 tpsHCI or 95% of the throughput of the baseline, non-compliant run in Fig. 3. So some of the performance loss was due to having 5 Tiles.

5   Data Accessibility Test

5.1   Impact on Performance During the Benchmark Run

In this set of experiments, we deliberately set the database cache size to be very small relative to the working set size (WSS) to exaggerate the impact of the accessibility test on the database performance.

In the first experiment, there is a lot of data on the server which is powered off. The data shows that aggressive re-synchronization can impact the database transaction rate.

The trade-off is that the resynchronization takes place very quickly and thus data is protected sooner than if the re-synchronization were less aggressive. The benchmark mandates that a chart showing the impact to transaction rate, as well as the overall recovery time is included in the Full Disclosure Report (FDR). The IOPS charts are not part of the FDR since IO is not measured directly from the workload generator (Fig. 7).

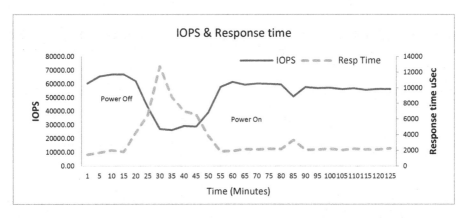

Fig. 7. The "spare" Node is powered off at minute 24 and powered back on at minute 48. The storage response time spikes and IOPS drops as the back-end re-synchronizes the missing data. Once the Node is powered back on the synchronization work ends – but replica data is now imbalanced, and the response time is slightly increased.

In the second experiment, there is relatively little data to synchronize. Thus, the impact on storage response time is much less because there is little work for the storage layer to do (Fig. 8).

As you would expect the impact on TPS is also much lower. These two experiments show that the impact to the database transaction rate is highly sensitive to the layout of data, in particular how much data resides on the Node which is powered off, and how aggressive the HCI system is when it resyncs that data (Figs. 9 and 10).

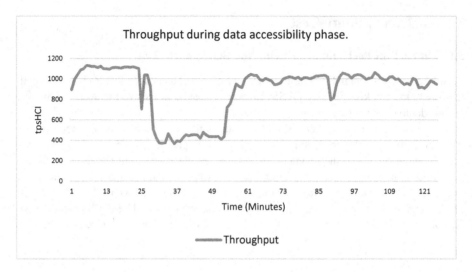

Fig. 8. Impact of the loss of a Node on throughput, when Node is full of data. The TPS drops immediately when the Node is powered off. We can clearly see that this configuration is reliant on the underlying storage for performance.

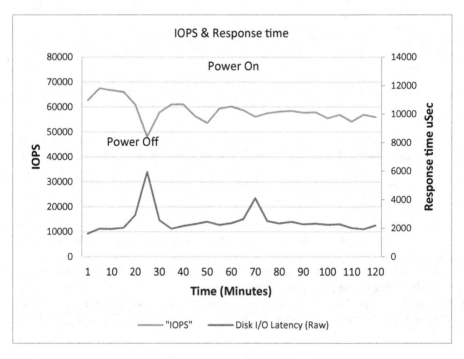

Fig. 9. Impact of the loss of a Node on IOPS and latency, with little data to synchronize

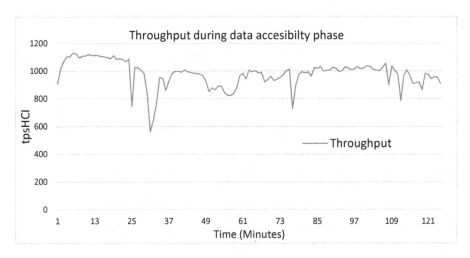

Fig. 10. Impact of the loss of a Node on throughput, with little data to synchronize

5.2   Recovery Activity After the Benchmark Run

Not all systems will choose to begin replication work immediately after the Node is powered off. Such a design choice will generate very low impact to the DB transactions. In fact, performance may improve as data is simply no-longer replicated to the down Node. Of course the trade-off is that user data is unprotected. In such cases we need to measure the time taken to re-replicate the data once the downed Node re-joins the cluster. The full disclosure report includes the time taken to reach full data-protection but does not measure the impact to transactions, since the recovery is after the benchmark run has competed.

6   Future Work

We should add measurement to the post-accessibility phase so that the impact to front-end work can be measured as well as the overall time to reach the fault-tolerance policy specified by the user.

7   Conclusions

We demonstrated that the TPCx-HCI benchmark can be used to showcase several properties of HCI systems: uniform access to data from all Nodes; convergence of compute, storage and networking; a cluster-level scheduler to balance the load across avilable servers; ability to tolerate the loss of a Node; speed of recovery and regaining of resilience. The benchmark does not directly demand these properties, but the workload and the run-time procedures are designed such that efficiencies in these areas are rewarded.

References

1. Bond, A., Kopczynski, G., Taheri, H.R.: Two firsts for the TPC: a benchmark to characterize databases virtualized in the cloud, and a publicly-available, complete end-to-end reference kit. In: Nambiar, R., Poess, M. (eds.) TPCTC 2012. LNCS, vol. 7755, pp. 34–50. Springer, Heidelberg (2013). https://doi.org/10.1007/978-3-642-36727-4_3
2. Bond, A., Johnson, D., Kopczynski, G., Taheri, H.R.: Architecture and performance characteristics of a PostgreSQL implementation of the TPC-E and TPC-V workloads. In: Nambiar, R., Poess, M. (eds.) TPCTC 2013. LNCS, vol. 8391, pp. 77–92. Springer, Cham (2014). https://doi.org/10.1007/978-3-319-04936-6_6
3. Bond, A., Johnson, D., Kopczynski, G., Taheri, H.R.: Profiling the performance of virtualized databases with the TPCx-V benchmark. In: Nambiar, R., Poess, M. (eds.) TPCTC 2015. LNCS, vol. 9508, pp. 156–172. Springer, Cham (2016). https://doi.org/10.1007/978-3-319-31409-9_10
4. Sethuraman, P., Reza Taheri, H.: TPC-V: a benchmark for evaluating the performance of database applications in virtual environments. In: Nambiar, R., Poess, M. (eds.) TPCTC 2010. LNCS, vol. 6417, pp. 121–135. Springer, Heidelberg (2011). https://doi.org/10.1007/978-3-642-18206-8_10
5. SPECvirt_sc2013 benchmark info, SPEC Virtualization Committee. http://www.spec.org/virt_sc2013/
6. TPC: TPCx-V benchmark. http://www.tpc.org/tpcx-v/default.asp
7. VMware, Inc., VMmark 3. http://www.vmware.com/products/vmmark/overview.html
8. VMware, Inc., vSphere Distributed Resource Scheduler. https://www.vmware.com/products/vsphere/drs-dpm.html

Requirements for an Enterprise
AI Benchmark

Cedric Bourrasset[1], France Boillod-Cerneux[1], Ludovic Sauge[1],
Myrtille Deldossi[1], Francois Wellenreiter[1], Rajesh Bordawekar[2(✉)],
Susan Malaika[2], Jean-Armand Broyelle[2], Marc West[2], and Brian Belgodere[2]

[1] BULL ATOS, 396 rue du mas de verchant, 34000 Montpellier, France
cedric.bourrasset@atos.net
[2] IBM Corporation, 1101 Kitchawan Road, Yorktown Heights, NY 10598, USA
bordaw@us.ibm.com
https://atos.net/fr/produits

Abstract. Artificial Intelligence (AI) is now the center of attention for
many industries, ranging from private companies to academic institutions. While domains of interest and AI applications vary, one concern
remains unchanged for everyone: How to determine if an end-to-end AI
solution is performant? As AI is spreading to more industries, what
metrics might be the reference for AI applications and benchmarks in
the enterprise space? This paper intends to answer some of these questions. At present, the AI benchmarks either focus on evaluating deep
learning approaches or infrastructure capabilities. Unfortunately, these
approaches don't capture end-to-end performance behavior of enterprise
AI workloads. It is also clear that there is not one reference metric that
will be suitable for all AI applications nor all existing platforms. We will
first present the state of the art regarding the current *basic* and *most
popular* AI benchmarks. We will then present the main characteristics of
AI workloads from various industrial domains. Finally, we will focus on
the needs for ongoing and future industry AI benchmarks and conclude
on the gaps to improve AI benchmarks for enterprise workloads.

1 Introduction

In the last decade there have been many changes in AI technology and the
use of AI. It has now emerged from the niche use, to enterprise use. This is
due to a few reasons: advances in AI algorithms, large advances in hardware
compute power, and the existence of massive amounts of data. Advancement in
AI algorithms and software as illustrated in Fig. 1, accelerated and took place
in the last decade. AI uses much of the same hardware technology that was
developed for HPC, which has seen very large increase of computing power.
Some of the increase is partly due to the availability of accelerator technology,
which suits Deep Learning workloads. Additionally, HPC has progressed the
capabilities and power to handling huge volumes of data in a high-performance
manner, AI consumes huge amounts of data so these advances in hardware are

© Springer Nature Switzerland AG 2019
R. Nambiar and M. Poess (Eds.): TPCTC 2018, LNCS 11135, pp. 71–81, 2019.
https://doi.org/10.1007/978-3-030-11404-6_6

the second area that hardware is enabling AI to advance. The final reason that AI has advanced is the large amounts of data to mine or train the algorithms is available. Think of the volumes of data each of us are generating as we use our smart phones or surf the World Wide Web, and that data is being captured. In addition, there are now so many 'connected' devices from manufacturing plant floors, to retail systems, to automobiles collecting data. Data by itself has little value until you can extract the information from it; which is where AI is playing a very important and significant role. Now that AI is being used in commercial production use, companies are having to evaluate what AI systems they will invest in. They have to build appropriate rationale and justification why they purchase one system versus another. This is no easy task as there are multiple hardware and software components that make up these systems. It would be nice to have a single standard test that would score a full AI system on its ability to run a given type of AI Enterprise workload. Unfortunately, the only way today to properly perform a comparative evaluation between AI Systems is to create a custom benchmark test suite based on the user's specific AI workload and data, and then invest the time and arrange access to the equipment to run the benchmark test suite on each of the systems under consideration. This paper will look at the metrics for Enterprise workloads, benchmark tests that are available, and then the gaps which need to be filled. This paper will look at what are those metrics for Enterprise workloads, what benchmark tests are available, and then the gaps which need to be filled.

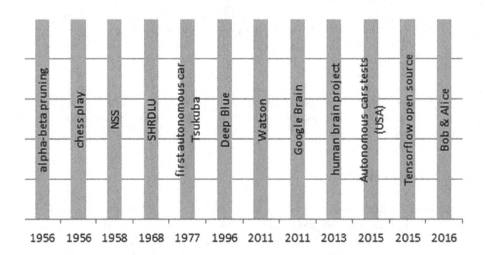

Fig. 1. AI major project and discoveries

2   Identification of AI Workflow Bottlenecks

The definition of standard AI benchmark metrics that are useful, relevant and sustainable requires first and foremost to identify the representative workloads of the implementation projects and the maintenance of an end-to-end AI solution in their widest diversity. These workloads must necessarily be selected for their criticality and their importance in the dimensioning in time (duration of the development project and fluidity of the life cycles) and in costs (infrastructure and software platform) of the project.

Most of the techniques used to address modern AI issues are based on recent academic and industrial advances in Machine Learning, which includes Deep Learning (ML/DL). The latter consists of using algorithms that create numerical models from datasets (supervised model training - when the training dataset include the true values for the variables to predict - or else unsupervised), which are then able to correctly predict results from new data.

These algorithms and typology of models are numerous and for reference one can quote here some of the most known for the supervised learning: Decision Tree, Logistic Regression, Bayesians Classifier, SVM (Support Vector Machine), and the large family of supervised DNN (Deep Neural Nets) used in Deep Learning: CNN (Convolutional Neural Networks), RNN (Recurrent Neural Networks). For unsupervised learning: K-means, hierarchical clustering, PCA (Principal Component Analysis), and specifically for DL: RBM (Restricted Boltzman Machine), auto-encoder, GAN (Generative Adversarial Networks), Word Embedding, and NNLM (Neural Net Language Model).

The model type and the training dataset size condition greatly the workload, as well as the system they run best on. For instance, GPUs are considered as cost effective solutions for standard Machine Learning models Training (Decision Trees, PCA, SVM) if the training datasets are large enough. On the other hand, the modern DL frameworks almost experience great performance speedup with GPUs during DL models Training and Inference phases compared to CPUs.

The life cycle of supervised ML/DL models is usually broken down into two phases: Training and Inference (sometimes called Prediction).

Training Phase

In the training phase, we usually identify:

- The preparatory stage. It generally includes the data gathering, the data preparation and the annotation/labeling of this dataset, the model choice and underlying characteristics, the feature engineering, and the technical choice for development and execution conditions of the training (ML/DL framework, programming language, physical platform). Otherwise, the model choice and the dataset size usually influence the platform and the framework selection as some framework environments are specialized for specific model training (for example: Python sklearn covers many Machine Learning model training, but limited for large datasets which Spark MLlib is then a good solution, Keras could train most of the Neural Nets models but pyTorch could be more flexible for LSTM models).
- The iterative stage of model training and optimization of the hyperparameters (parameters of the chosen models and the training algorithm) until reaching the desired model accuracy. This iterative cycle often goes

back to the preparation stage if the dataset is incomplete or has flaws or if the engineering features or model choice must be reviewed or the technical environment of the training execution has reached a hard limit that blocks the whole process.

The preparation phase depends very strongly on human factors. The data preparation stage is one of the critical steps of the process and is entirely under human supervision (often subject matter experts) and their total automation is almost impossible. However, some sub-steps can be automated. One can cite for example: the data-augmentation, the data denoising, the data formatting/reformatting, the signal pre-processing and the data fusion (Compute vision, Acoustic, Lidar point clouds), the data semi-auto labeling. The duration of the cycle of training and optimization of the hyper-parameters is dominated by two factors: the training time of the models which is by far the heavier and longer machine time and the faculty to quickly find the values of the hyper-parameters which maximizes the model accuracy. The technical preparation stage also depends on the context, plus human and organization choices. The optimization of hyper-parameters is often performed by experienced data scientists and there exist optimum search techniques and tools that automate this task.

Inference Phase

The inference phase depends first and foremost on the targeted deployment platform: this concerns data center servers or on the edge devices (embedded systems, smart camera, smart phone, embedded card in vehicles or robots). Their platform characteristics are primarily for the Inference Performance: presence or not of hardware AI Accelerators, RAM capacity, CPU, IO, OS, framework, types of sensors, process performances and energy consumption, etc.). These factors strongly condition the parameters of the stage of model packaging to adapt them to the targeted deployment platform. This could include the model reduction to adapt to the platform hardware footprint (memory size, compute capacity, energy consumption), response time performance improvement, the integration of data pre-processing and post-processing logics, and some extra logical processing workflow (including calling other models) and then packaging in a secured format compatible with the target deployment platform. Finally comes the model deployment followed by the solution run-time and exploitation with the objective of achieving the desired performance in the conditions and constraints of actual operation in terms of model prediction accuracy and end-to-end processing time.

Another important stress factor to consider for the Training and Inference platforms is related to the level of workload concurrency introduced by parallel incoming requests. This could be illustrated for the Training phase, when several users share the same training platform and may concurrently submit intensive Training tasks. For the Inference phase, it is also very likely that several incoming detection requests have to be proceed by a platform at the same time.

At this stage, we can now identify three AI tasks which are good candidates for platform benchmarking: Model Training, Hyper-parameter Optimization and Deployed Model Inference Run-time. For each of them, we identify in Table 1 their workload profile, propose some Important Performance Indicators to assess the tasks efficiency, and potential Technical Bottleneck which could limit the AI tasks performance delivered by a given solution.

3 Desired Enterprise AI Metrics

3.1 Important Characteristics of Enterprise Metrics

The question about how to define good benchmarks and good metrics is a question which has been extensively discussed and debated for decades. Example of an industry-standardized benchmark is the one developed and maintained in the compute domain by the Standard Performance Evaluation Corporation (SPEC) organization [12]. SPEC defines a computer benchmark as a benchmark that performs a known set of operations by which computer performance can be measured and this with the following characteristics [12]:

– Specifies a workload
– Produces at least one metric
– Is reproducible
– Is portable
– Is comparable
– Has run rules.

Enterprise benchmark workloads must be of course be representative of real or typical production workloads running in standard and effective production conditions. These workloads must exercise extensively all the components of the solution as-a-whole (hardware, software = ecosystem including the frameworks) and the key performance elements composing the solution (CPU, memory, IO, Network,) in the same time. It does differ from our point of view from standard synthetic benchmark where key performance components are more exercised spectrally as for instance in the HPC domain with HPL/LINPACK for the CPU [5,6,9], memory with McCalpin's STREAM benchmark [1,8], OSU for the interconnect [3] and HPC Challenge (HPCC) [7] which is designed to measure a range memory access patterns.

Another class of metrics of interest to enterprises is related to best value for money. It includes for instance the TCO metric (Total Cost of Ownership). TCO is a widely used metric to support acquisition and planning decisions of standard computing installation. TCO includes:

– Investment costs or Capital expenditure (CAPEX) for investments made upfront: hardware, software, data center construction costs
– Operational costs or expenditure (OPEX) for recurring costs: energy costs, human resources, maintenance.

Table 1. Characterization of AI tasks

AI tasks	Workload profile	Important performance indicators	Potential technical bottlenecks in standalone scenario	More potential technical bottlenecks with concurrent scenario
Model training	Batch task	Trained models, duration of the training process, scalability of the training mechanism is any	GPU memory capacity and latency/bandwidth, GPU compute capabilities and capacities	Platform ability to efficiently manage the systems resources and schedule AI training workload (similar to HPC workload management tool benchmark)
	GPU intensive workload	Price-performance metrics: in regard to TCA/TCO	GPU-CPU and CPU-RAM communication characteristics could matter for large dataset training and/or Out-of-GPU-memory training	GPU-CPU communication characteristics could matter for large datasets
	Minutes to days	For concurrent scenario, the level of model training concurrency (similar to batch concurrency benchmark)	Server-server communication characteristics could matter for intra-parallelism model training (training a single model across multiple servers)	CPU-RAM communication characteristics could matter for Out-of-Core training
Hyper-parameter optimiza-tion	Batches tasks managed by a workload orchestrator and hyper-parameters solver	Hyper-parameter combinatorial values to cover	Solver algorithm limitations	All the model training potential bottleneck apply here as well
	GPU-tasks	Optimum value found for the model accuracy	All the model training potential bottlenecks apply here	
	Minutes to days	Overall duration to find the model with the best hyper-parameters		
Deployed model inference run-time	Online service or library API	Latency of inference	GPU latency, GPU compute capabilities and capacities	Platform ability to efficiently manage the systems
	Toward real-time request response-time in most cases. Milli-seconds to seconds	Price performance metrics: in regard to TCA and or TCO	GPU-CPU and CPU-RAM latency and throughput	
	Mostly hardware AI accelerator intensive workload (GPU, FPGA, neuromorphic chip, embedded solutions)	For embedded and/or autonomous systems: energy consump-tion/performance metric	Infrastructure network communication characteristics	
		For concurrent scenario, the level of model training concurrency (similar to OLTP metrics)		

3.2   End-to-End AI Performance Metrics

In recent years, the Artificial Intelligence realm has exploded in a wide range of domains such as natural language processing, image and video recognition, fraud detection, text translation, autonomous car driving, fire prevention, stellar classification, business intelligence and so on so forth. All these domains deal with heterogeneous data types and a more and more complex paradigms and models, such as Map Reduce, Convolutional Neural Network, Recurrent Neural Network with a large variety of flavors. At the same time, these domains have to manage their own constraints, consume as little power as possible, be real-time, be precise, or a mix of these. Potentially, complex systems have different constraints at different levels and separate them altogether, e.g. smart cameras can capture videos and preprocess them to send more relevant data to another model located in a datacenter that will generate information to the screen of an operator. For that large set of purposes, these last years have seen the emergence of several hardware utilization coming from different horizons, such as HPC (GPUs, low latency fabrics, rapid and large storage arrays, NUMA machines with hundreds of computation cores and large memory areas), embedded systems (FPGA), or newly designed ASICs dedicated to matrix or vectorized computation (Google TPU, Intel Nervana). These devices have been selected for specific purposes, some for optimizing specific computations, others for their parallelism capabilities, other for data vectorization, others high data throughput, optimizations for atypic data types, data exchange with low latency, or large data capacity. At the same time, a wide range of frameworks were being developed to implement efficiently different paradigms enabling as much specific hardware access as possible.

To compare results and give sense to them, the choice of the metrics is therefore crucial. One simple metric is of course the time-to-solution approach. Time-to-solution is highly depending on the runtime conditions of the benchmark and also about the accuracy level of the final result. For standard industry benchmarks, as we focus on production, we need to consider optimizing throughput (work completed per a period of time and system) rather than simple time-to-solution; focusing only on the best as possible time-to-solution generally leads to underuse of the system so wastes computing resources. In addition, these metrics only make sense if we consider accuracy level of the trained model (quality metric). Therefore, time-to-accuracy and throughput-to-accuracy.

Energy/power consumption is more and more important for environmental and economic reasons. Energy consumption is generally hard to measure but a close approximation is the computation time, considering that the power per operation ratio is almost constant with electronic devices. Consequently, computation time should be measured as an indication of energy efficiency.

In Sect. 2 it was identified there are three AI tasks which need to be focused on for platform benchmarking: Model Training, Hyper-parameter Optimization and Deployed Model Inference Runtime. Indeed, they are time critical in the overall AI process and their progress does not require human intervention. For each of them we identified in Table 1 their workload profile, proposed some Important

Performance Indicators to assess the tasks efficiency, and potential Technical Bottleneck which could limit the AI task's performance delivered by a given solution.

The huge diversity of the features, and sometimes conflicting needs, of existing and future AI models clearly show that only measuring a unique parameter for a given benchmark set is not sufficient at all and would not objectively reflect the computation capabilities of an AI system. Therefore, the scoring value must be determined by a function of other measured characteristics. For example, let us consider a benchmark measuring the training phase of a deep learning related model implementing natural language processing, if hardware A reaches 0.999 in one hour and hardware B 0.99 in 1 s, which one may score better? A function such as the following would be a good function.

$$score = -log_{10}(1 - accuracy)/time \tag{1}$$

First of all, why such parameters have been chosen? The answer is quite complex to address, each domain having a large (and sometimes conflicting) variety of targets and constraints:

- Real-time latency
- Computation accuracy
- Convergence speed
- Computation time
- Computation efficiency
- Hardware resource consumption
- Thermal conditions
- Power capping
- Energy consumption.

The list above is absolutely not exhaustive and proves that a restrictive set of parameters might not measure definitively all the possible cases. However, if we look deeper into the different measurements, there does exist a common denominator. As a summary, a good AI oriented system is a system that produces a given accuracy in the shorter time slot and with as little energy as possible.

Secondly, the problem of mixing these parameters together to produce a score reflecting the performance quality of a system is not trivial. Let us consider in the text below the following:

- $error = 1\text{-}accuracy$ (the lower that $error$ is, the better)
- $freq = \frac{1}{time}$ (the larger $freq$ is, the better)
- $eval$ is the scoring function we would like to estimate.

The idea is that $eval$ is a function of $error$ and $freq$, and we want to consider are variations of these values, i.e., the partial derivatives. For simplicity reasons, we limit ourselves to first order polynomials and quotients and express that the slope of the evaluation function must not vary with $freq$, but increase when the $error$ decreases. Since $\frac{\partial eval}{\partial error} \approx \frac{1}{\partial error}$ and $\frac{\partial eval}{\partial freq} \approx 1$. Therefore,

$eval(error, freq) = K \times log(error) \times freq$ (where K is a constant). We can also set $K = -1i$ (since $error$ is under 1, log will be negative), and the resulting formula is:

$$eval(time, accuracy) = \frac{-log(1 - accuracy)}{time}$$

4 Related Work

DeepBench [10] from Baidu Research was one of the first initiatives for benchmarking AI workloads. This benchmark targets the low-level operations that are fundamental to deep learning, such as matrix-multiplication, convolutions, and communications, and aims to measure which hardware provides the best performance on the basic operations used for deep neural networks. It also evaluates forward and backward pass time during training time for a subset of existing networks (CNN, LSTM). These measurements are useful for identifying bottlenecks in deep learning training and inference for hardware and software development but fails to address specific issues of the Enterprise. Similar to DeepBench, Tensorflow [2] provides a set of benchmarks focusing on throughput performance for many well-known CNN networks. While these measurements can provide information on pure throughput evolution from one hardware platform to another, it is currently limited by the lack of considerations regarding model accuracy when addressing Enterprise issues and is tied to the TensorFlow framework. DAWNBench [4] is a Stanford University led project designed to allow different deep learning methods to be compared by running a number of competitions. It was the first major benchmark suite to examine end-to-end deep learning training and inference. DAWNBench provides a reference set of common deep learning workloads across multiple domains (currently image classification (on ImageNet, CIFAR10) and question answering (on SQuAD) as of DAWNBench V1) for quantifying training time, training cost, inference latency, and inference cost across different optimization strategies such as model architectures, software frameworks, clouds environments, and hardware platforms. While the cost and latency information are useful to the Enterprise in deciding how and where to build their solution, it fails to address the data preparation and hyperparameter optimization work which accounts for a significant portion of time to solution within an Enterprise compared to the final training time of a model with well optimized hyper-parameters and thoroughly and correctly labeled well represented data set of a given task. Following the precedent of DAWNBench competition style, MLPerf defines the primary [11] metric as the wall clock time to train a model to a target quality, often hours or days. The target quality is based on the current state of the art publication results, less a small delta to allow for run-to-run variance. In addition, MLPerf reports cloud service costs and power consumption, as a proxy for cost, for mobile or on premise systems. MLPerf [11], aims to provides a comprehensive benchmarking suite, covering both training and inference tasks, for measuring the performance of machine learning software frameworks, hardware accelerators, and cloud platforms. The suite expands on DAWNBench's workloads and common Machine Learning tasks is defined by a well-known public dataset and quality target as follows:

1. Image Classification – Resnet-50 v1 applied to Imagenet.
2. Object Detection – Mask R-CNN applied to COCO.
3. Speech Recognition – DeepSpeech2 applied to Librispeech.
4. Translation – Transformer applied to WMT English-German.
5. Recommendation – Neural Collaborative Filtering applied to MovieLens 20 Million (ml-20m).
6. Sentiment Analysis – Seq-CNN applied to IMDB dataset.
7. Reinforcement Learning – Mini-go applied to predicting pro game moves.

Each task is further divided into two distinct divisions, Closed and Open Model. The MLPerf Closed Model Division specifies the model to be used and restricts the values of the hyper parameters (batch size, learning rate, etc.) which can be tuned to enforce a fair and balance comparison of the hardware and software systems. The MLPerf Open Model Division, only requires that same task must be achieved using the same data, but provides fewer restrictions. Similar to DAWNBench, MLPerf's Closed Division provides the Enterprise with guidance on deciding how and where to build solutions, but fails to address the issues with regard to data preparation and hyper-parameter optimization work. The Open Division provides the Enterprise with a view in advances in current state of the art research, but fails to map to the Enterprise.

5   Summary and Next Steps

Artificial Intelligence has moved from academia and research, to many commercial workloads. Companies are making purchasing decision for suitable AI solutions to meet their enterprise AI workload needs. As we learned, enterprise AI workloads have a broad and unique set of requirements for performance metrics. Analysis of the existing benchmarks revealed gaps between the current existing benchmarks, and the important metrics that enterprises want to measure for their AI workloads. We discussed key metrics and areas of study that are of concern to AI enterprise clients. These include:

- Model Training performance
  - data labeling/preparation
  - time-to-accuracy
  - computational time/cycles
  - throughput
- Hyper-parameter optimization performance
- Inference runtime performance.

As a summary, a good AI oriented system is a system that produces a given accuracy in the shortest time slot and with as little energy as possible. But for enterprise systems with concurrent users and workloads, not just the shortest time is required but the overall throughput of the system. Finally, there are multiple aspects of the system to test making comparison difficult, so we proposed a formula to reduce to an overall score.

Our conclusion is that there is a need to fill and the community needs to develop additional benchmarks or expand existing benchmarks. Not only that, we need to drive to a set of standard benchmarks, which then AI system vendors can test their solutions against, making it much easier for commercial customers to evaluate and compare solutions before making their purchase decision.

References

1. The Stream benchmark. https://www.cs.virginia.edu/stream
2. Abadi, M., et al.: TensorFlow: a system for large-scale machine learning. In: Proceedings of the 12th USENIX Conference on Operating Systems Design and Implementation, OSDI 2016, pp. 265–283. USENIX Association, Berkeley (2016). http://dl.acm.org/citation.cfm?id=3026877.3026899
3. DKP et al.: OSU micro-benchmarks. http://mvapich.cse.ohio-state.edu/benchmarks
4. Coleman, C.A., et al.: DAWNBench: an end-to-end deep learning benchmark and competition. In: Proceedings of the 31st Conference on Neural Information Processing Systems (NIPS 2017) (2017)
5. Dongarra, J.J., Heroux, M.A., Luszczek, P.: HPCG benchmark: a new metric for ranking high performance computing systems. Technical report UT-EECS-15-736, November 2015
6. Heroux, M.A., Dongarra, J.J., Luszczek, P.: HPCG technical specification. Technical report SAND2013-8752, October 2013
7. Luszczek, P., et al.: S12 – the HPC challenge (HPCC) benchmark suite. In: Proceedings of SC 2006, November 2006
8. McCalpin, J.D.: Memory bandwidth and machine balance in current high performance computers. In: IEEE Computer Society Technical Committee on Computer Architecture (TCCA) Newsletter, December 1995
9. Petitet, A., Whaley, R.C., Dongarra, J.J., Cleary, A.: HPL - a portable implementation of the high-performance Linpack benchmark for distributed-memory computers. http://www.netlib.org/benchmark/hpl/
10. Bench Research: Deep Bench (2018). https://github.com/baidu-research/DeepBench
11. Bench Research: ML Perf (2018). https://mlperf.org/
12. SPEC. https://www.spec.org/cpu2017/Docs/overview.html

Towards Evaluation of Tensorflow Performance in a Distributed Compute Environment

Miro Hodak and Ajay Dholakia[(✉)]

Lenovo, Data Center Group, Morrisville, NC, USA
{mhodak, adholakia}@lenovo.com

Abstract. Tensorflow (TF) is a highly popular Deep Learning (DL) software framework. Neural network training, a critical part of DL workflow, is a computationally intensive process that can take days or even weeks. Therefore, achieving faster training times is an active area of research and practise. TF supports multiple GPU parallelization, both within a single machine and between multiple physical servers. However, the distributed case is hard to use and consequently, almost all published performance data comes from the single machine use case. To fill this gap, here we benchmark Tensorflow in a GPU-equipped distributed environment. Our work evaluates performance of various hardware and software combinations. In particular, we examine several types of interconnect technologies to determine their impact on performance. Our results show that with the right choice of input parameters and appropriate hardware, GPU-equipped general-purpose compute clusters can provide comparable deep learning training performance to specialized machines designed for AI workloads.

Keywords: Tensorflow · Deep learning · GPU · Distributed computing
Performance

1 Introduction

Tensorflow (TF) [1] has quickly become the most popular Artificial Intelligence (AI) software framework available. It has been developed and contributed to the open-source community by Google, which continues to maintain control over the code. The popularity of TF in comparison to other AI software frameworks is evident in metrics such as Stack Overflow queries, GitHub stars, and number of forks. Its closest competitor appears to be Facebook-backed PyTorch [2], which has recently seen significant surge in adoption.

In general, the training of deep learning frameworks, especially convolutional neural networks (CNNs), is a highly computationally demanding task. Large data sets are needed, e.g., ImageNet, an often used labeled dataset that contains millions of images and is hundreds of GBs in size [3]. Furthermore, training CNNs to an acceptable accuracy target requires days or even weeks [4]. What makes this problem worse is that training often times requires adjusting several parameters and thus researchers developing new

© Springer Nature Switzerland AG 2019
R. Nambiar and M. Poess (Eds.): TPCTC 2018, LNCS 11135, pp. 82–93, 2019.
https://doi.org/10.1007/978-3-030-11404-6_7

models need to repeat training multiple times. Overall, the model training phase of AI software development process can often run into months if not longer.

One way of addressing a high computational cost is using GPUs, which are efficient in performing computational operations used in AI training. The idea of using GPUs is becoming so well established by now that most AI tutorials simply assume that user has access to high performing GPUs. TF, for example, defaults to using a GPU if available.

Even with high performing GPUs, training times are still considerable and as a result, multi-GPU training is becoming commonplace. The hardware infrastructure with multiple GPUs can be designed either by using a single computer equipped with multiple GPUs (scale-up) or by using multiple computers with GPUs (scale-out). While TF supports both scenarios, the scale up case has become far more common. This is probably due to two main factors: (i) it makes parallelizing easier (no need to support many different types of network connections) and (ii) a single machine guarantees high-speed communication between GPUs. This has led to rising popularity of specialized hardware for AI workloads containing multiple GPUs within a single machine connected with a high speed interconnect. Two examples are DGX-1 [5] and DGX-2 [6] developed by Nvidia, consisting of 8 and 16 GPUs, respectively, connected via NVLink [7].

Yet this approach also has disadvantages: specialized hardware is very costly compared to general use compute servers and at some point scale-out becomes more practical than scale-up as is the case in the high performance computing (HPC) world. Outside of TF, the power of the scale-out approach has been demonstrated by several recent studies: Facebook researchers who showed that training using 32 servers with 256 GPUs can reduce ImageNet training time to only about an hour [8], while another study demonstrated distributed training in ~ 15 min [9].

Within TF, there are several obstacles for distributed training to become commonplace. The main one is that current TF distributed model requires substantial changes to the training script while single-machine parallelization requires much less effort. In addition, adoption of distributed TF is limited by existing documentation being aimed at expert users familiar with concepts of parallel computing rather than targeting data scientist audience. Furthermore, distributed TF does not easily integrate with job schedulers used to launch jobs in compute clusters.

Motivated by these challenges, our work aims to evaluate performance of distributed TF from the point of view of a typical AI user and to provide an easy-to-follow guidance for achieving good performance in a distributed environment. To this end, we use unmodified TF binaries as provided by the project along with publicly available benchmarking scripts. Our work examines multiple hardware and software factors to identify those that are critical in a distributed environment.

We find that network connection speed is the most important parameter determining scaling efficiency. At minimum, a 10 Gb Ethernet is needed to achieve good scaling, but higher speeds provide additional performance benefit. Additionally, large batch sizes are also desirable. With these two parameters, a performance comparable to that of AI specialized servers can be achieved.

The rest of the paper is organized as follows. Section 2 summarizes related research work being undertaken by teams at many academic as well as industry organizations Sect. 3 outlines various considerations required for effective model training using distributed frameworks at various levels of the hardware and software system stack and also calls out the need for appropriate user skills to achieve the task. Section 4 presents the results of the work described in this paper. Finally, Sect. 5 outlines areas of ongoing and future research and summarizes the conclusions.

2 Related Work

Speeding up training of deep neural networks is an active area of recent research. Many teams have investigated software techniques as well as system designs for reducing the training time.

In [8], the authors investigated the use of large minibatch sizes on systems with up to 256 GPUs and reported training CNNs for ImageNet classification in one hour. This is a significant improvement over prior published results where as many as 29 h were needed. The authors also deployed a new warmup scheme as part of the learning rate schedule to overcome certain optimization difficulties encountered when using larger than typical minibatch sizes.

In [9], the authors developed a more sophisticated approach to learning rate adaption along with the use of very large minibatch sizes. This approach, named Layer-wise Adaptive Rate Scaling (LARS) algorithm, allowed use of large minibatch sizes (such as 32 K) on a system with 1024 CPUs and resulting in a reported training time of 14 min.

Cho et al. [10] have developed a distributed deep learning library named PowerAI DDL. The library implements a multi-ring communication pattern that can achieve a nearly linear scaling for up to several hundred GPUs. It also provides a good balance between latency and bandwidth for various hardware configurations. Compared to Ref. [8], the authors claim a lower communication overhead. This library has been integrated into Tensorflow, Caffe and Torch.

Compared to these works, we take a different approach to distributed deep learning. Instead of developing new software, we focus on how to efficiently use existing distributed framework implemented in TF. Also, we use small clusters containing up to 16 GPUs that should constitute most common use cases.

3 Distributed TF Performance Considerations

3.1 Distributed Model Support in TF

There are two paradigms for distributing AI training workloads: data and model parallelisms [11]. In model parallelism, each compute device executes part of the model using the same data. For example, each device may be responsible for training different layers of the network. Implementing model parallelism is generally complex and model dependent.

Data parallelism, which is used in present work, is much more common. Here, each compute device executes the same model with a different subset of the data. TF uses a concept of "parameter servers" and "workers". Workers are compute devices - GPU or

CPU – that perform computationally intensive part of the training to obtain partial gradients. Those are sent to parameter servers that communicate with each other to calculate global gradients.

3.2 Hardware

At hardware level, performance is mainly determined by two factors: (i) GPU processing power and (ii) interconnect between GPUs. The former is straightforward and is given by GPU type. For example, V100, the highest performing GPU currently available, provides 12.3 TFLOPS of single precision operations and 112 TFLOPS at half precision.

As for GPU communication, the current intra-machine standard is PCIe. NVLink, a proprietary interconnect often used in AI-specialized servers, provides several times higher bandwidth. In a distributed settings, interconnect between servers also comes into play. Here we only consider Ethernet because it is the only network communication protocol officially supported in TF. However, it is not an optimal choice, because Ethernet protocol has a high latency compared to Infiniband and other high-speed fabrics that are used for HPC applications. Several Ethernet types are available for compute clusters with speeds ranging from 1 Gb/s to 100 Gb/s. Non-Ethernet interconnects, such as Inifiniband or Omni-Path, can also be configured to carry Ethernet communication and thus can also be used for distributed TF.

Clearly, NVLink-based machines provide a much higher communication speed than PCIe/Ethernet distributed clusters. Nevertheless, the distributed case can still provide a comparable performance if the GPU computational time is much higher that the communications cost. CNNs, which are computationally intensive, may be such a workload.

3.3 Job Scheduler

Job scheduler is a critical component of distributed computing environments. It ensures that workloads are executed on appropriate resources without interfering with each other. Unfortunately, TF distributed model does not integrate well with job scheduling software. This is because it requires specifying IP addresses of compute nodes at submit time, while job scheduler assigns nodes upon job execution according to availability. While it is possible to work around this issue, it is another hurdle for user when executing distributed TF jobs.

3.4 Libraries

The main compute libraries involved in neural network training are CUDA and cuDNN developed by Nvidia. In general, these provide good performance out-of-the box and there is not much user needs to do other than to ensure that installed version fully supports his/her GPUs.

3.5   Training Script

Training script controls setup and training of CNNs. Because of complexity of CNN design, most users elect to reuse and modify existing scripts as needed rather than writing one from scratch. For example, TF GitHub project Models (Tensorflow/ models) provides ready to use implementation of most commonly used CNN models. Many of these can run in distributed mode and accept input parameters such as batch size to adapt to existing hardware. Thus, while in principle training scripts give users full control over training execution and provide opportunities for performance tuning, these are usually not exercised.

3.6   User Expertise

While user expertise is important for any application, here we highlight it because running distributed TF workloads places a high burden on a user who needs to be an expert on AI, hardware and software simultaneously. While AI expertise may be implicitly assumed, the level of required software and hardware skills seems too high for a typical data scientist. On software side, user needs to be able write a parallel training script. However, even when using an already existing script, user needs to use the right options for parameter servers and replicated variables. Furthermore, because TF distributed model does not provide support for launching training jobs on multiple nodes, user also needs to be able to write his/her own script launching simultaneous training sessions on the computational nodes in the cluster. On the hardware side, user needs to be aware of networking setup: IP addresses need to be explicitly specified and, as will be shown below, he/she needs to utilize a high speed Ethernet interconnect to achieve efficient distributed training.

These issues originate in TF itself and thus it is up to TF community to make distributed training easier to use. Otherwise, these features will remain inaccessible to most users and/or a separate fork or a wrapper (such as Hovorod developed by Uber [12]) will become standard for distributed deployments.

4   Results

4.1   Hardware and Software

This study was performed on an 8 node Lenovo ThinkSystem SD530 [13] compute cluster. Each node contained 2 Intel® Xeon® Gold 6150 CPUs and 400 GB of total memory. Additionally, each node also had 2 GPUs connected via PCIe 3.0. V100 GPUs were used to generate main results reported in Sect. 4.2, while for comparison to Nvidia DGX-1 results (Sect. 4.3) the V100 GPUs were replaced by P100 GPUs. Various types of network connections between compute nodes were utilized in this work as listed in Table 1.

TF version 1.8 with CUDA, as provided by TF Docker Hub, was used for this work. The docker container was converted into singularity container format, which is preferable for cluster environment, and the benchmarks were run from within a singularity container.

Table 1. Ethernet connections in the cluster: nominal and actual bandwidths (as measured by *iperf3* utility).

Connection type	Nominal bandwidth [Gb/s]	Actual bandwidth [Gb/s]
1 Gb Ethernet	1	0.94
10 Gb Ethernet	10	9.41
Omni-Path IPoIB	100	32.1

Performance was measured using TF benchmarking suite available from GitHub (tensorflow/benchmarks). Specifically, tf_cnn_benchmark.py script located in scripts/tf_cnn_benchmark directory was used. The script is often used within TF community as a way to verify and compare performance of various hardware configurations. Importantly, it comes with bundled synthetic training data, which greatly simplifies deployment. The script is designed according to TF recommendation for achieving high performance [14]. TF projects publishes its own results for several types of GPUs [15], which allows users to verify that they are getting expected performance from their hardware.

The script reports number of processed images per second, effectively a measure of processing bandwidth. The script accepts a number of command line options allowing users to easily select a deep learning model, batch size, number of steps as well as options controlling execution on multiple GPUs and compute nodes.

4.2 Optimum Parameters for TF Distributed Training

TF benchmark script provides several options for controlling variable distribution and gradient aggregation. Two most important ones are *parameter_device* and *variable_update*. The former can have two values: *cpu* or *gpu*, while the latter has three possible options: *replicated* (single node only), *parameter_server*, and *distributed_replicated* (multi-node only). We have tested all possible combinations of these settings for 1, 2, and 4 GPUs and the results are shown in Tables 2, 3 and 4, respectively. Based on the results we use *gpu/replicated* for 1 GPU training, *cpu/parameter_server* for 2 GPU 1 node training, and *gpu/parameter_server* for multi-node training.

Table 2. Performance of settings controlling variable distribution and gradient aggregation for resnet50, batch size 64 on 1 V100 GPU.

Parameter device	Variable update	Images/second 32 bit precision	Images/second 16 bit precision
CPU	parameter_server	344	574
CPU	replicated	347	596
GPU	parameter_server	347	599
GPU	replicated	349	596

Table 3. Performance of settings controlling variable distribution and gradient aggregation for resnet50, batch size 64 on 2 V100 GPUs (1 node).

Parameter device	Variable update	Images/second 32 bit precision	Images/second 16 bit precision
CPU	parameter_server	690	1181
CPU	replicated	677	1170
GPU	parameter_server	656	1093
GPU	replicated	663	1148

Table 4. Performance of settings controlling variable distribution and gradient aggregation for resnet50, batch size 64 on 8 V100 GPUs (4 nodes).

Parameter device	Variable update	Images/second 32 bit precision	Images/second 16 bit precision
CPU	parameter_server	2200	3353
CPU	distributed_replicated	2280	3447
GPU	parameter_server	2300	3527
GPU	distributed_replicated	1903	2560

4.3 Distributed Benchmarks

Benchmark scaling studies were performed on up to 16 V100 GPUs. The results in terms of processed images per second are shown in Figs. 1, 2 and 3 for batch sizes of

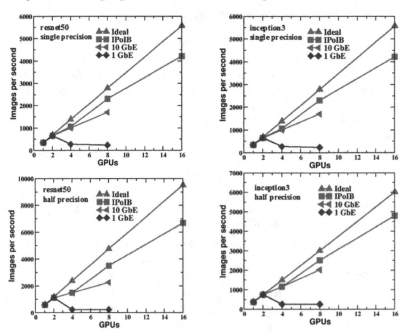

Fig. 1. ResNet-50 (left) and Inception-v3 (right) V100 benchmarks for batch size of 64. Each line corresponds to different network speed as given in the legend. Ideal dataset is a single GPU performance multiplied by number of GPUs.

64, 128, and, 256, respectively. ResNet-50 and Inception-v3 models are used with both single (32 bit) and half (16 bit) precisions. Due to hardware limitation, only the IPoIB benchmark extends to 16 GPUs, all other cases are limited to 8 GPUs.

Datasets are sorted according to network speed with datapoints labeled "Ideal" representing 100% scaling. These are obtained by multiplying single GPU performance by number of GPUs.

Figure 1 displays results for the smallest batch size used in this study – 64. This is the most challenging case for the cluster environment, because GPU computational is relatively short and thus the communication cost becomes more evident. The results show that with the 1GbE speed the performance drops after when more than 1 node become included in the calculation. This is clearly insufficient for this workload. 10 GbE, on the other hand, fares much better and shows a performance increase. At 8 GPUs the 1GbE scaling efficiency is between about 50–75%. Omni-Path fabric in IP mode provides a substantial improvement with efficiencies between 70–88% on 16 GPUs depending on the model and precision.

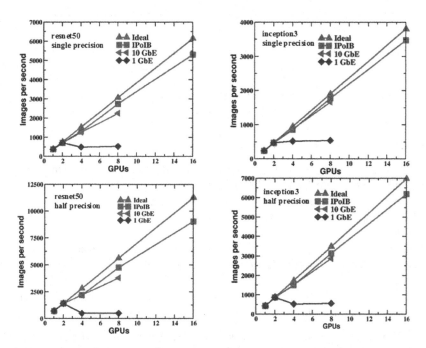

Fig. 2. ResNet-50 (left) and Inception-v3 (right) V100 benchmarks for batch size of 128. Each line corresponds to a different network speed as given in the legend. Ideal dataset is a single GPU performance multiplied by number of GPUs.

The scaling accuracy improves with a batch size of 128 as shown in Fig. 2. While 1GbE remains insufficient for the workload, 10 GbE scaling efficiency improves to 70–80% over 8 GPUs and Omni-Path IPoIB efficiency is 80–90% over 16 GPUs.

Figure 3 shows results for batch size 256. Because of memory requirements, only half precision can be used on the GPUs at this batch size. Here, the performance becomes even closer to an ideal scaling with 10 GbE providing 80 and 90% efficiency for ResNet-50 and Inception-v3, respectively at 8 GPUs. Onmi-Path IPoIB is scaling at about 90% at 16 GPUs for both models. Note that 10GbE is competitive with IPoIB over the tested range.

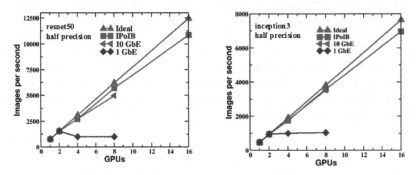

Fig. 3. ResNet-50 and Inception-v3 (right) V100 benchmarks for batch size of 256. Each line corresponds to a different network speed as given in the legend. Ideal dataset is a single GPU performance multiplied by number of GPUs.

4.4 Discussion

The results reveal several trends:

- High-speed network connection is crucial for achieving speedup when increasing number of nodes. At least 10 Gb/s is necessary
- Larger batch sizes provide better scaling performance
- More computationally intensive model (Inception-v3) provide better scaling performance
- Half precision worsens the scaling for a given batch size. However, when run with maximum batch size possible, the scaling mirrors that of single precision at its maximum batch size
- When combining large batch sizes with a high speed network, PCIe/Ethernet clusters provide a highly scalable deep learning platform

The important role of network speed was recognized in previous studies. For example, all related works cited in Sect. 2 use Inifiniband interconnect. Ref. [8] even estimates that a 15 Gb/s network speed is required for ResNet-50 training on P100 GPUs. Given that V100 can perform more operations than P100, the network speeds need to be higher in V100 compute clusters. Using their formula, we can estimate that about 20 Gb/s would be needed for single precision training, while half precision, which is much improved in V100 s, would require about 75 Gb/s. While our results show that these estimates are too high, they further demonstrate the need for network speed in distributed deep learning training.

Yet, this point is not mentioned in user TF documentation, which may give users impression that any network speed is sufficient. Indeed, several Issues in TF Benchmarks GitHub page have been opened about distributed training not yielding any speedup.

Our findings indicate that higher batch sizes provide better performance. This is because increasing batch size increases GPU calculation time relative to the time spent on communication between parameter servers. This reasoning suggests that users should always maximize batch size up to maximum allowed by GPU memory size. However, users should also be mindful of the fact that excessive batch sizes – over 512 for Imagenet data – lead to lower accuracy [16] and, in practice, users should always check accuracy of their models and carefully balance processing speed vs model accuracy. That said, current generation of GPUs come in 16 GB and 32 GB variants, which allow maximum Imagenet batch sizes of 256 and 512, respectively for 16 bit precision. Therefore, using close to a maximum batch size should be a safe choice for training Imagenet-based models on P100 and V100.

It is also important to compare our data with performance obtained from scale-up servers. TF project has published performance data from an 8 P100 DGX-1 server, in which GPUs are connected by an NVLink connector, on its website [15]. To facilitate a direct comparison, we have repeated previous benchmarks on P100 GPUs. The results show that for ResNet-50, the difference is 7% at 8 GPUs and 10% for Inception-v3.

No such data is available for V100, but Nvidia has published ResNet-50 performance of DGX-1 with 8 V100 [17]. They found that for batch size 256 and using half-precision 5183 images/second can be processed. Our value, shown in Fig. 3, left panel, is 5536. The difference likely comes from a different TF or Cuda version, or a different training script - the source document does not provide detailed information on how the benchmark was performed. Nevertheless, the values are close and this further demonstrates value of compute clusters for AI workloads.

5   Conclusions and Future Work Directions

The goals of this work have been to evaluate TF performance in a distributed setting and compare it to that of AI-specialized integrated clusters that are currently popular for deep learning workloads. Distributed TF use case is not well documented and our work provides practical guidelines for achieving good performance. These are:

1. High speed network connection is crucial. At least 10 Gb needs to be used, the higher the speed, the better.
2. Maximize batch size.
3. Use appropriate settings for variable distribution.

Following these rules, scaling efficiency of about 90% over 16 top-of-the-line GPUs can be achieved for deep learning training. This demonstrates that general-purpose compute clusters provide performance that is comparable to that of tightly integrated servers specifically designed for AI workloads. Given that AI-specialized machines are very costly, distributed computing provides better value when used according to the rules outlined above.

Our investigation also shows why integrated machines are popular for AI work-loads: Both writing and executing distributed scripts within TF is hard and requires advanced computing skills. This needs to change to make distributed training accessible to the data scientist community.

Future work will further explore different Ethernet speeds to provide a clear network speed recommendation for CNN training. Additionally, direct communication over a high-speed fabric – Infiniband and Omni-Path – using direct memory access (DMA) will also be tested. By default, TF only supports Ethernet communication, but VERBS implementation, providing DMA, is also part of TF codebase and can be enabled by compilation from source. Another option is the Hovorod library [12], which effectively turns TF into an HPC application. These will decrease network latency and increase bandwidth and thus are expected to further improve performance.

Another direction is making TF easier to use in a compute cluster environment such as better scheduler integration so that users can easily leverage it for their AI training needs.

Finally, a better understanding of distributed TF performance is a stepping stone towards using benchmarks such as very recently released MLPerf [18] so that different types of hardware can be evaluated in a predictable manner.

References

1. Abadi, M., et al.: TensorFlow: a system for large-scale machine learning. OSDI **16**, 265–283 (2016)
2. Paszke, A., et al.: Automatic differentiation in PyTorch. https://openreview.net/forum?id=BJJsrmfCZ
3. Imagenet. http://image-net.org/about-stats
4. Chatfield, K., Simonyan, K., Vedaldi, A., Zisserman, A.: Return of the devil in the details: Delving deep into convolutional nets. arXiv preprint arXiv:1405.3531 (2014)
5. Nvidia Corporation. https://www.nvidia.com/en-us/data-center/dgx-1/
6. Nvidia Corporation. https://www.nvidia.com/en-us/data-center/dgx-2/
7. Nvidia Corporation. https://www.nvidia.com/en-us/data-center/nvlink/
8. Goyal, P., et al.: Accurate, large minibatch SGD: training imagenet in 1 hour. arXiv preprint arXiv:1706.02677 (2017)
9. You, Y., Zhang, Z., Hsieh, C., Demmel, J., Keutzer, K.: ImageNet training in minutes. CoRR, abs/1709.05011 (2017)
10. Cho, M., Finkler, U., Kumar, S., Kung, D., Saxena, V., Sreedhar, D.: PowerAI DDL. arXiv preprint arXiv:1708.02188 (2017)
11. Goodfellow, I., Bengio, Y., Courville, A., Bengio, Y.: Deep Learning, vol. 1. MIT Press, Cambridge (2016)
12. Sergeev, A., Del Balso, M.: Horovod: fast and easy distributed deep learning in TensorFlow. arXiv preprint arXiv:1802.05799 (2018)
13. Lenovo SD530. https://lenovopress.com/lp0635-thinksystem-sd530-server
14. Tensorflow Performance Guide. https://www.tensorflow.org/performance/performance_guide
15. Tensorflow P100 Benchmarks. https://www.tensorflow.org/performance/benchmarks#results

16. Mishkin, D., Sergievskiy, N., Matas, J.: Systematic evaluation of convolution neural network advances on the Imagenet. Comput. Vis. Image Underst. **161**, 11–19 (2017)
17. NVIDIA DGX-1 With Tesla V100 System Architecture. http://images.nvidia.com/content/pdf/dgx1-v100-system-architecture-whitepaper.pdf
18. MLPerf. https://www.mlperf.org/

A Comparison of Two Cache Augmented SQL Architectures

Shahram Ghandeharizadeh$^{(\boxtimes)}$ and Hieu Nguyen

USC Database Laboratory, Los Angeles, USA
{shahram,hieun}@usc.edu

Abstract. Cloud service providers augment a SQL database management system with a cache to enhance system performance for workloads that exhibit a high read to write ratio. These in-memory caches provide a simple programming interface such as get, put, and delete. Using their software architecture, different caching frameworks can be categorized into Client-Server (CS) and Shared Address Space (SAS) systems. Example CS caches are memcached and Redis. Example SAS caches are Java Cache standard and its Google Guava implementation, Terracotta BigMemory and KOSAR. How do CS and SAS architectures compare with one another and what are their tradeoffs? This study quantifies an answer using BG, a benchmark for interactive social networking actions. In general, obtained results show SAS provides a higher performance with write policies playing an important role.

Keywords: Caching · Write policy · Scalability · Performance

1 Introduction

Cache Augmented Database Management Systems (CADBMSs) are a proven technology deployed widely by popular social networking sites such as Facebook [35], Tinder, and Wikipedia. These caches require an application developer to identify a code path or a method (function) with a unique input as a key and its results as a value [20,25,35,37]. Next, the code path is extended to look up the key. If the cache returns a value then the application consumes the value without executing the code path. Otherwise, it executes the code path to generate the corresponding key-value pair and inserts this key-value in the cache for future look up. In the presence of updates to the database, the application may either delete (termed *write-around* or invalidate) or update the impacted key-value pairs (termed *write-through* or refill). These are similar to the write-around and write-through techniques of host-side[1] caches [10,26,29,30].

There is a spectrum of software architectures for CADBMSs. We term the two extreme ends of this spectrum as the Client-Server (CS) and the Shared-Address Space (SAS) architectures. Both provide a simple interface such as get,

---

[1] A key difference is that the write is manipulating key-value pair instead of a disk/SSD block.

© Springer Nature Switzerland AG 2019
R. Nambiar and M. Poess (Eds.): TPCTC 2018, LNCS 11135, pp. 94–109, 2019.
https://doi.org/10.1007/978-3-030-11404-6_8

insert/put, delete, increment, decrement, and others. Moreover, both may use leases such as those proposed by [22] to prevent undesirable race conditions that cause the cache to generate stale data.

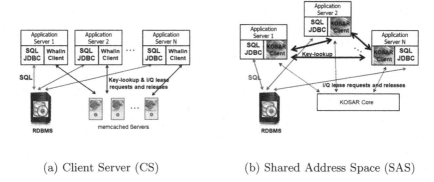

(a) Client Server (CS)   (b) Shared Address Space (SAS)

Fig. 1. Two alternative architectures for cache augmented database management systems.

With CS, there are stand-alone cache manager processes per server. Examples include memcached [34,43] and Redis [38]. Figure 1a shows this architecture for memcached. An application server uses memcached's client component, Whalin Client [43], to issue requests to an instance of memcached process executing on a memcached server[2]. With multi-core servers, a cache server may host multiple[3] memcached processes, each process is termed a *cache manager instance*. The memory of the cache server is partitioned across these instances. Cache entries would be represented as key-value pairs and assigned to different instances of memcached. This might be realized by partitioning key-value pairs using either a hash function, by assigning ranges of keys, or a hybrid of the two [1].

With SAS, the cache manager is a library that runs in the address space of an application, see KOSAR Client of Fig. 1b. This library manages memory and implements a replacement technique such as LRU. We use the term *cache manager instance* to refer to an instance of the library running as a part of an application node. A coordinator implements leases, see KOSAR Core of Fig. 1b. As depicted in Fig. 1b, the cache manager instances may communicate and collaborate with one another to facilitate key-lookup. Different cache manager instances may reference and compute the same key-value pair independently. A coordinator, KOSAR Core, maintains consistency between different cache manager

---

[2] A physical server may host both the Application and memcached processes. We use such a deployment to evaluate CS architecture in Sect. 5.

[3] While memcached is multithreaded, launching multiple instances reduces contention for its synchronization primitive on its LRU queue. In our experiments with a 16 core processor, we have observed a 20% enhancement in throughput when launching eight instances instead of one.

instances. Examples of SAS architecture include Java Cache standard [27] along with its Apache Ignite [5] and Google Guava [24] implementations, Terracotta BigMemory [41], JBoss [11] and KOSAR [17]. Both Java Cache standard and Google Guava are single node implementations and lack the concept of a coordinator.

While hybrids of CS and SAS are possible, this study focuses on CS and SAS only[4].

Software architecture of SAS and CS are fundamentally different. With CS, there is a cache manager client and a cache manager server that communicate via message passing. SAS combines these two into one with a published interface for use by the application server. Moreover, it has a coordinator that grants leases to prevent undesirable race conditions that insert stale data in the cache.

The architectural differences cause CS and SAS to process read and write requests differently. With CS, a read that looks up the value of a key incurs the network overhead to issue the request to a cache manager instance. This is in the form of serializing the command and transmitting it across the network back to the client. If the cache manager instance finds the value then it serializes the value and transmit it across the network. SAS avoids this network overhead every time an application node finds its referenced key in the memory of its local cache manager. With SAS, writes manipulate the in-memory representation of a key-value pair. With CS, these writes incur the network overhead of transmitting the key-value pair similar to reads.

A key question is how CS and SAS architectures compare with one another? And, do they scale horizontally? The **primary** contribution of this study is an answer to these questions using KOSAR [17] as the representative of the SAS architecture[5] and IQ-Twemcached [21] as a representative of the CS architecture[6]. While we acknowledge the availability of other candidate systems, we selected KOSAR and IQ-Twemcached because they are the only systems that implement leases of [22] to provide strong consistency. To elaborate, both CS and SAS architectures suffer from undesirable race conditions that insert stale data in the cache [22]. Leases of [22] detect these race conditions and prevent them from causing the state of the cache and the database to diverge.

While both KOSAR and IQ-Twemcached may be configured to control the number of key-value replicas across the cache, we configured IQ-Twemcached in its simplest form where clients hash partition key-value pairs with no replication. We configured KOSAR such that each client may construct a replica of its referenced key-value pair. This means that with N cache manager instances, KOSAR may have N replicas of a popular key-value pair in each instance while

---

[4] Evaluation and comparison of a hybrid with CS and SAS is deferred to future work, see Sect. 6.

[5] At the time of this writing, Google Guava is not distributed and could not be used for this evaluation. Apache Ignite is a candidate for future analysis, see Sect. 6.

[6] Redis is the other obvious alternative that we intend to include in our future studies, see Sect. 6.

IQ-Twemcached has at most one replica of the same key-value pair in one cache manager instance.

CADBMSs are designed for workloads that exhibit a high read to write ratio. Examples include social networking applications with Facebook reporting 500 reads for every 1 write [9] and enterprise systems trending towards read-dominated workloads [14,31]. For this evaluation, we use a macro benchmark that emulates interactive social networking actions [7] and generate read-heavy workloads.

Our evaluation highlights the following main lessons:

1. SAS provides a higher performance than CS. However, CS scales better than SAS for some workloads.
2. Choice of a write policy (write-around versus write-through) impacts both the performance observed with each architecture and their scalability characteristics. The write-through policy provides superior performance and scalability characteristics when compared with write-around. However, its resulting software is more complex, see [19].
3. One may configure client components of a SAS architecture in either a greedy or a cooperative mode. In the greedy mode, each client manages its key-value pairs independent of the other clients. In the cooperative mode, a client with a replica of a key-value pair $(k_i\text{-}v_i)$ services another client's cache miss for k_i. Our evaluation shows cooperative is superior to greedy with write-around, enhancing both the performance and scalability of the SAS architecture. With write-through, there is little difference between greedy and cooperative. See Sect. 4.
4. Both architectures scale sub-linearly even with a 1000:1 read to write ratio and a handful of nodes. While scalability of SAS is limited by the processing capability of the RDBMS server, scalability of CS is limited due to load imbalance across cache manager servers.

All performance numbers presented in this paper are gathered using a cluster of servers. Each server is a 4 (8 hyper-threaded) core Intel i7-3770 3.40 GHz CPU with 16 GB of memory, a 1 Gbps networking card, and a 1 Terabyte disk.

The rest of this study is organized as follows. We describe related work in Sect. 2. Section 3 provides an overview of the BG benchmark and its implementation using write-around and write-through techniques. While the write-around implementation is similar with CS and SAS, we present a fine-tuned implementation of write-through for each of CS and SAS architectures. Section 4 quantifies the performance benefits of using a cooperating technique to manage the content of caches with SAS, showing it is key to scaling SAS. Section 5 compares the CS and SAS architectures using their performance and scalability characteristics. Our conclusions and future research directions are detailed in Sect. 6.

2 Related Work

In a data center deployment, caches may be deployed either inside or outside the RDBMS. Caches outside the RDBMS include host-side caches [10,26,29] and application-side caches [20,25,35,37]. Caches inside the RDBMS include the buffer pool manager of a RDBMS server [28,33,36,39], client-side [13,15,42] and mid-tier [8,32] caches.

Host-side, RDBMS server, client-side and mid-tier caches are transparent to an application. Host-side caches are deployed seamlessly using a storage stack middleware or the operating system (termed the caching software) [10,26,29]. They stage disk pages from disk to NAND Flash to expedite their processing. The RDBMS server cache may employ algorithms such as LRU [12], LRU-K [36] and its queue based implementation [28], and ARC [33] to manage buffer frames occupied by disk pages [39]. Client-side caches [13,15,42] distribute the processing of the algebraic operators that constitute a query across both the client and server component of a RDBMS. They ship data to a client for caching and processing. The book by Franklin [15] provides a survey of these caches. Mid-tier caches offload part of a workload to intermediate database servers that partially replicate data from the backend server [8,32]. These may cache entire tables, materialized views, or query fragments, providing distributed query execution.

This study considers application-side caches that are external to the RDBMS and managed by the application. These caches provide a simple get, insert, delete, increment, decrement interface and have no query processing ability. We evaluate a non-transparent version of these caches. Our initial attempt to evaluate a transparent version of one of these caches produced results that we could not explain. A future research direction is to revisit this cache and others similar to it in light of the lessons learned from this study to explain their performance and scalability characteristics.

In [2], we compare a host-side cache named Flashcache with an application-side cache based on the CS architecture (IQ-Twemcached [22]). The same IQ-Twemcached is used in this study. This study is different because we compare two application-side caches based on different software architecture with one another, namely, KOSAR and IQ-Twemcached.

One finds studies and white papers on the web comparing the CS and SAS architectures with one another. However, to the best of our knowledge, this study is the first to compare the CS and SAS architectures scientifically. We show the application's use of write-around and write-through policies impact the final conclusions. This level of analysis is lacking from the studies available on the web.

3   A Social Networking Benchmark

We use BG [4,7], a benchmark that produces interactive social networking actions, to evaluate the alternative caching architectures. Rows of Table 1 show the seven BG actions that constitute our focus. Three of these actions read data while the other four write data. The read actions are View Profile, List Friends, and View Pending Friend requests. The write actions are Invite Friend, Reject Friend Request, Accept Friend Request, and Thaw Friendship. We configure BG with three different mixes of these actions that emulate a different ratio of read to write actions, varying from 10:1 to 1000:1, see Table 1. According to [9], the ratio of read to write actions at Facebook is 500:1.

We used the Social Action Rating (SoAR) metric of BG to compare the SAS and CS architectures with one another. SoAR is the highest throughput observed from the system while satisfying a service level agreement, SLA. In all our experiments, the SLA was set at 95% of actions observing a response time faster than 100 ms with no anomalies [3]. An anomaly refers to either stale, inconsistent, or simply erroneous data produced by the system. This metric is quantified during the validation phase of BG.

Table 1. Three interactive social networking workloads.

BG social actions	Read to write ratio		
	1000:1	100:1	10:1
View Profile	33.3%	33%	30%
List Friends	33.3%	33%	30%
View Friend Req	33.3%	33%	30%
Invite Friend	0.04%	0.4%	4%
Accept Friend Req	0.02%	0.2%	2%
Reject Friend Req	0.02%	0.2%	2%
Thaw Friendship	0.02%	0.2%	2%

The three read actions of BG emulate a socialite either viewing the profile of a member, listing her friends, or listing her pending friend requests. The referenced member may be the same as the socialite, e.g., viewing her own profile or list of friends. View Profile retrieves the profile of the referenced member and includes the member's number of friends. If this is a self reference then the number of pending friend invitations of the member is also retrieved. List Friends shows the profile of ten friends of a member. Similarly, List Pending Friends shows the profile of ten members who have extended a friendship invitation to the referenced member.

The four write actions pertain to social activities that members may perform on one another. These actions are also invoked by a socialite on another member. They are self explanatory based on their names and we refer the interested reader to [7] for the details.

BG is a stateful benchmark in that it only generates valid actions. For example, it does not emulate a socialite to extend a friend invitation (using Invite Friend Request) to another member if they are already friends. Similarly, a socialite performs Thaw Friendship on a member who is a friend of that socialite. To prevent the social graph from either running out of friendships (for the Thaw Friendship action) or members to invite (for the Invite Friend Request), we ensured the mix of write actions is symmetric so that friendships are thawed and created with the same probability, see Table 1.

BG uses a closed emulation model to generate request where a thread emulates a socialite picked using a Zipfian distribution of access. We used 0.27 as the exponent of the distribution to generate a skewed pattern of reference where 30% of members serve either as socialites or referenced members by 70% of generated actions.

The version of BG used in this study is different than [7] in that all BGClients share[7] one social graph to generate requests, see Integrated DataBase (IDB) of [4]. This ensures different application servers incur read-write, write-read, and write-write conflicts. We used the feature of BG to detect anomalies (stale, erroneous, or simply wrong) to verify the two architectures implement actions correctly.

With write-around, both the representation of key-value types and their management is identical with the alternative architectures. However, an implementation of write-through with CS is different than with SAS. We fine-tune the representation of key-value pairs with SAS because its implementation of read-modify-write (RMW) incurs a lower overhead than CS.

In [19], we provide implementation details of BG actions with write-around and write-through. This discussion includes use of Inhibit (I) and Quarantine (Q) leases [22] are applied to prevent insertion of stale values in the IQ-Twemcached. Due to lack of space, we refer the interested reader to [19] for details.

4   Cooperative Cache Management

With SAS, a cooperating cache management technique has a significant impact on system performance and its scalability. This is specially true with write-around even when there is enough memory to materialize all key-value pairs in the cache.

Two cache management techniques supported by KOSAR are Greedy and Ingest. Greedy is non-cooperative and requires each cache to manage its content using its local replacement policy independent of the other caches. This means a cache that observes a miss for a key-value pair must compute this key-value pair using the RDBMS even though as many as $N - 1$ replicas may exist in the other caches. With the RDBMS as the slowest component, once an update impacts a popular key-value pair and invalidates it, this key-value pair is potentially re-computed N times. Once by each cache that observes a miss for it. This causes the cache servers to wait for the RDBMS, limiting the scalability of the system.

Ingest, on the other hands, is a cooperative cache management technique. It ensures a key-value pair is computed by at most one cache. Other caches that observe a miss for this key are directed to fetch it from the cache that has a

---

[7] The version of BG described in [7] partitions a social graph into N logical subgraphs and assigns each to a BGClient for request generation. It fails to evaluate the SAS architecture objectively because its request generation results in no read-write and write-write conflicts between different BGClients, i.e., emulated application servers of Fig. 1.

replica of it. In essence, each cache may serve as a producer of a key-value pair missed by another cache as long as the producer has a copy of the referenced key.

KOSAR implements Ingest as follows. Its Core maintains a list of caches (KOSAR Clients of Fig. 1b) with a copy of a key-value pair. When a KOSAR Client requests an I lease (due to a cache miss) on a key, the Core provides it with the list of KOSAR Clients that have a replica of this key. The KOSAR Client selects one of these randomly, fetches a replica of its required key-value pair, and releases its I lease. The Core decides whether the client may maintain this copy or not based on the allowed number of replicas[8].

Figures 2a–c show SoAR of Greedy and Ingest with write-around and write-through techniques. The x-axis shows the number of clients. The scale of the y-axis changes in these figures, highlighting a significant difference in SoAR for different workloads. Greedy and Ingest provide a comparable performance with write-through because each experiment has a warmup phase and write-through updates key-value pairs instead of deleting them. With write-around, Ingest is superior to Greedy. With a 10:1 read to write ratio, Greedy provides a lower SoAR as we increase the number of BG clients beyond 1 to 2 and higher, see Fig. 2a. This results in a system with a poor scalability characteristics, see Fig. 2d. In particular, the observed SoAR with 8 nodes is less than half that observed with 1 node. With 1 node, the CPU of the application server is 100% utilized. With 8 nodes, the CPU of the RDBMS server is 100% utilized. Every time a write action invalidates a popular key-value pair, Greedy requires each cache to compute it independently. This imposes a higher load onto the RDBMS as a function of additional caches. Processing of requests using RDBMS is slower than looking up results in the cache, causing the SoAR with 8 nodes to be lower than that with one node.

With a 1000:1 workload, Greedy supports a higher SoAR from 1 to 4 clients. Its SoAR drops sharply from 4 to 8 clients. The explanation for this is similar to the above with the system switching from the application server being 100% utilized with 1 node to the RDBMS becoming 100% utilized with 8 nodes. A key observation is that a lower frequency of writes enhances the scalability of Greedy.

By computing a key-value pair only once independent of the number of cache servers, Ingest enables write-around to provide similar performance to write-through. However, the scalability of Ingest is limited with read to write ratios of 10:1 and 100:1 as the RDBMS must process transactions that use SQL DML commands to implement the write actions. The RDBMS becomes the bottleneck with all configurations to limit system scalability. For example, with 10:1, both the RDBMS disk and CPU are heavily used. Disk shows a sustained queue of 1.25 elements (a 100% sustained utilization) and the CPU is more than 80% utilized. The cache servers are idle most of the time waiting for the RDBMS to finish processing the write actions. Hence, increasing the number of cache servers does not enhance system SoAR, see Fig. 2d.

---

[8] Release and notify are performed with 1 message.

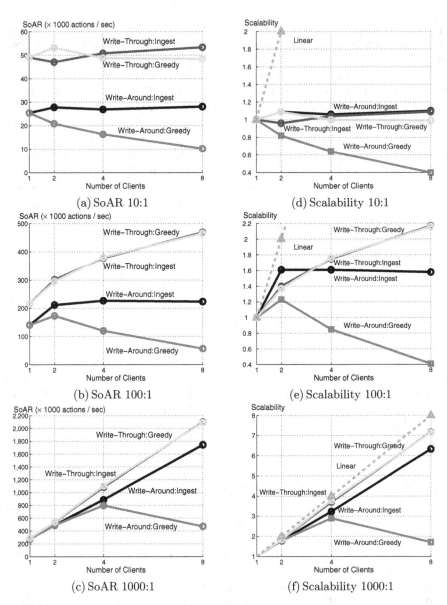

Fig. 2. Performance and scalability of SAS architecture (KOSAR), 100K member social graph, 10 friends and 0 resources per member. The scalability with different number of clients is computed relative to the SoAR observed with 1 client, scalability with x clients $= \frac{SoAR(x)}{SoAR(1)}$. With one client, scalability is 1.

5   A Comparison of CS with SAS

This section compares IQ-Twemcached (CS architecture) with KOSAR configured using Ingest (SAS architecture). We report on both system SoAR and
its scalability characteristics. With the CS architecture, there is a pairing of
BGClients with the IQ-Twemcached. Hence, with a single BGClient, there is no
physical network transmission because the IQ-Twemcached and the BGClient
issuing requests are on the same server. However, with 2 and more nodes,
the BGClients hash partitions the key-value pairs across the IQ-Twemcached
instances. As detailed in Sect. 5.2, the network overhead incurred with two or
more nodes impacts the scalability of the CS architecture when compared with
a single node. This is particularly true with 100:1 and 1000:1 workloads.

We start with a single node comparison of the two architectures. Subsequently, we analyze the scalability of each architecture.

5.1   Single-Node Comparison

Table 2 shows SAS is superior to CS by providing a higher SoAR with different
workloads. Both architectures enhance the performance of a RDBMS by itself,
compare column 2 with the other columns. A higher read to write ratio enhances
the performance of both caching solutions. Moreover, write-through outperforms
write-around by re-filling the impacted key-value pairs instead of deleting them.
The SoAR of SAS/KOSAR is 5 to 9 folds higher than CS/IQ-Twemcached with
100:1 and 1000:1 read to write ratios. This difference drops to 25%–60% with a
10:1 read to write ratio because the RDBMS disk becomes 100% utilized with
SAS and limits its performance.

Table 2. SoAR with a single cache node as a function of read to write ratio of BG
actions. The resource that becomes the bottleneck is identified in parentheses below
the SoAR rating.

Read to write ratio	No cache SQL-X	Write-around		Write-through	
		CS IQ-Twemcached	SAS KOSAR	CS IQ-Twemcached	SAS KOSAR
10:1	12,227	20,300	25,436	29,898	49,004
	(RDBMS CPU)	(RDBMS CPU/Disk)	(RDBMS Disk)	(App Server CPU)	(RDBMS Disk)
100:1	18,516	26,916	140,857	41,509	215,850
	(RDBMS CPU)	(App Server CPU)	(App Server CPU)	(App Server CPU)	(App Server CPU)
1000:1	21,969	28,430	275,317	43,348	292,899
	(RDBMS CPU)	(App Server CPU)	(App Server CPU)	(App Server CPU)	(App Server CPU)

Table 2 shows the SAS architecture is generally more efficient than the CS
architecture. In particular, it does not incur the repeated overhead of fetching a

key-value pair using the network stack of the operating system and deserializing it to obtain the required value. Hence, SAS outperforms CS by a wide margin even though the CPU of the application server is the bottleneck resource with both architectures.

5.2   Scalability Comparison

Figures 3 and 4 show the SoAR and scalability of the different architectures with write-around and write-through, respectively. SAS is more scalable than CS only with the 1000:1 workload. While CS is more scalable than SAS with the 10:1 and 100:1 workloads, SAS provides either the same or a significantly higher performance (SoAR) than CS with all workloads. With the 10:1 workload, both CS and SAS architectures fails to scale. This is true with both the write-around and write-through policies, see Figs. 3d and 4d. The frequent writes cause the RDBMS to become the bottleneck with one cache manager instance and remain the bottleneck with additional instances. The RDBMS is busy processing the SQL DML commands (insert, delete, update) issued by the write actions. These transactions result in a sustained disk queue at the RDBMS server that limits scalability and dictates overall performance. Switching to SSD increases throughput. However, it does not change the scalability results because the throughput with one cache server would be higher (due to use of SSD). Below, we compare the scalability of different architectures with write-around and write-through in turn.

With write-around and a 100:1 workload, the CPU of the RDBMS server becomes 100% utilizes and limits the scalability of the SAS architecture[9]. The RDBMS is busy servicing queries generated by cache misses. These cache misses are attributed to write actions that delete cached key-value pairs. An increase to 1000:1 read to write ratio reduces the imposed load on the RDBMS to enable SoAR to scale. However, the RDBMS continues to remain the bottleneck, preventing SAS from scaling linearly.

With the CS architecture, the 1 Gbps network bandwidth of the individual application servers has a high utilization with 100:1 and 1000:1 workloads. The CPU utilization of the application servers is also high (>80%). The BGClients generate approximately the same amount of load on the IQ-Twemcached servers. This load is not evenly distributed across the IQ-Twemcached instances due to partitioning of the key-value pairs. This imbalance explains the sublinear scalability with the CS architecture. (The SAS architecture does not observe the same imbalance due to replication of key-value pairs.)

Write-through reduces the dependence of an architecture on the RDBMS by requiring the write actions to compute new key-value pairs. This reduces the number of queries issued to the RDBMS, enhancing the observed SoAR. With a 1000:1 read to write ratio, the SAS architecture scales almost linearly because the CPU of the different application servers is almost 100% utilized. With the CS architecture the network card of each node remains fully utilized to dictate both

---

[9] With 8 nodes, the average application server utilization is lower than 30%.

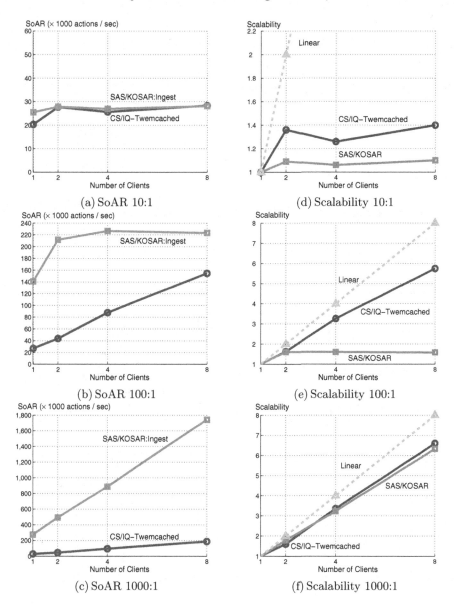

Fig. 3. A comparison of CS/IQ-Twemcached and SAS/KOSAR with write-around.

the SoAR of the system and its scalability. Similar to the discussion of write-around, CS does not scale due to load imbalance across the IQ-Twemcached instances[10].

---

[10] Similar results is reported by other systems that partition data [16, 23].

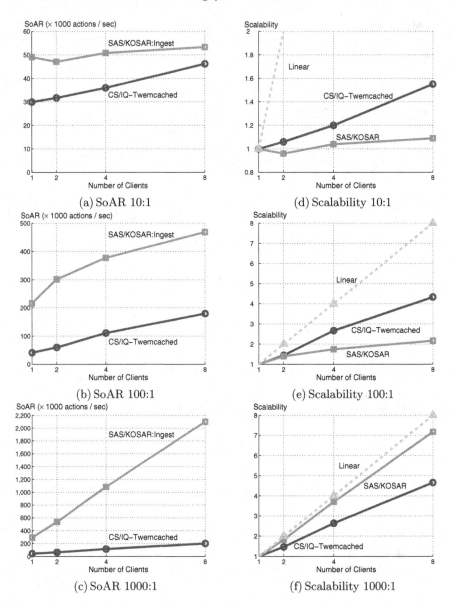

Fig. 4. A comparison of CS/IQ-Twemcached and SAS/KOSAR with write-through.

6   Conclusions and Future Research

Both SAS and CS architectures enhance the performance of a RDBMS dramatically for workloads with a high read to write ratio. The SAS architecture is higher performant than the CS architecture. SAS fails to scale linearly due to the RDBMS becoming the bottleneck. One approach to resolve this limitation is to deploy multiple RDBMS instances and shard a database across them [6]. Challenges of this design include additional design considerations to perform cross-shard filter or join, processing of transactions that update data in different fragments, and others as detailed in [40]. An alternative is to use a write-back policy that applies writes to the RDBMS asynchronously. An implementation of this policy may buffer writes in the caching layer. A challenge is how to process key-value references that observe a cache miss and issue a query to the RDBMS with pending buffered writes. The cache manager requires novel algorithms to apply the relevant buffered writes to the cache prior to processing the RDBMS query to compute the missing cache entry.

The evaluation presented in this study can be extended in several ways. First, this study considered only one sample system for SAS and one sample system for CS. A future effort is to expand this evaluation to include other sample systems such as Apache Ignite for SAS and Redis for CS. A key question is whether strong consistency is a requirement for an apple-to-apple comparison. Use of leases introduces delays that slows down performance. At the same time, strong consistency may not be required for applications such as social networking. We intend to investigate this tradeoff in greater detail.

Second, this study did not consider a hybrid of the CS and SAS architectures. Such an architecture may deploy the cache of CS with the coordinator of SAS, see KOSAR Core of Fig. 1a. This may enhance availability of data when application servers fail frequently. In general, analyzing failure of caches and its impact on the performance of alternative architectures is an open research topic.

Finally, we are aware of no study that has evaluated a write-heavy workload such as TPC-C with alternative write policies including write-back [18]. With these policies, a SAS architecture may provide a superior performance while preserving the ACID property of transactions.

Acknowledgement. We thank the anonymous reviewers for their valuable comments.

References

1. Adya, A., et al.: Slicer: auto-sharding for datacenter applications. In: OSDI, pp. 739–753 (2016)
2. Alabdulkarim, Y., Almaymoni, M., Cao, Z., Ghandeharizadeh, S., Nguyen, H., Song, L.: A comparison of Flashcache with IQ-Twemcached. In: IEEE CloudDM (2016)
3. Alabdulkarim, Y., Almaymoni, M., Ghandeharizadeh, S.: Polygraph: a plug-n-play framework to quantify anomalies. In: IEEE ICDE, April 2018
4. Alabdulkarim, Y., Barahmand, S., Ghandeharizadeh, S.: BG: a scalable benchmark for interactive social networking actions. Future Gener. Comput. Syst. **85**, 29–38 (2018)
5. Apache: Ignite - In-Memory Data Fabric (2016). https://ignite.apache.org/
6. Armstrong, T., Ponnekanti, V., Borthakur, D., Callaghan, M.: LinkBench: a database benchmark based on the Facebook social graph. In: ACM SIGMOD, June 2013

7. Barahmand, S., Ghandeharizadeh, S.: BG: a benchmark to evaluate interactive social networking actions. In: CIDR, January 2013
8. Bornhövd, C., Altinel, M., Krishnamurthy, S., Mohan, C., Pirahesh, H., Reinwald, B.: DBCache: middle-tier database caching for highly scalable e-Business architectures. In: Proceedings of the 2003 ACM SIGMOD International Conference on Management of Data, San Diego, California, USA (2003)
9. Bronson, N., Lento, T., Wiener, J.L.: Open data challenges at Facebook. In: 31st IEEE International Conference on Data Engineering, ICDE 2015, Seoul, South Korea, 13–17 April 2015, pp. 1516–1519 (2015)
10. Byan, S., et al.: Mercury: host-side flash caching for the data center. In: IEEE Symposium on Mass Storage Systems and Technologies (MSST) (2012)
11. JBoss Cache. http://www.jboss.org/jbosscache
12. Denning, P.J.: The working set model for program behavior. Commun. ACM **11**(5), 323–333 (1968)
13. DeWitt, D.J., Futtersack, P., Maier, D., Vélez, F.: A study of three alternative workstation-server architectures for object oriented database systems. In: Proceedings of the 16th International Conference on Very Large Data Bases, VLDB 1990 (1990)
14. Faust, M., et al.: Footprint reduction and uniqueness enforcement with hash indices in SAP HANA. In: Hartmann, S., Ma, H. (eds.) DEXA 2016. LNCS, vol. 9828, pp. 137–151. Springer, Cham (2016). https://doi.org/10.1007/978-3-319-44406-2_11
15. Franklin, M.J.: Client Data Caching: A Foundation for High Performance. Kluwer Academic Publishers, AH Dordrecht (1996)
16. Ghandeharizadeh, S., DeWitt, D.J.: A multiuser performance analysis of alternative declustering strategies. In: Proceedings of the Sixth International Conference on Data Engineering, Los Angeles, California, USA, pp. 466–475 (1990)
17. Ghandeharizadeh, S., et al.: A demonstration of KOSAR: an elastic, scalable, highly available SQL middleware. In: ACM Middleware (2014)
18. Ghandeharizadeh, S., Ngueyn, H.: Design, implementation, and evaluation of write-back policy with cache augmented data stores. Technical report 2018-06, USC Database Laboratory (2018)
19. Ghandeharizadeh, S., Nguyen, H.: A comparison of two cache augmented sql architectures. Technical report 2018-04, USC Database Laboratory (2018). http://dblab.usc.edu/Users/papers/CSvsSAS.pdf
20. Ghandeharizadeh, S., Yap, J.: Cache augmented database management systems. In: ACM SIGMOD DBSocial Workshop, June 2013
21. Ghandeharizadeh, S., Yap, J., Nguyen, H.: IQ-Twemcached. http://dblab.usc.edu/users/IQ/
22. Ghandeharizadeh, S., Yap, J., Nguyen, H.: Strong consistency in cache augmented SQL systems. In: Middleware, December 2014
23. Ghemawat, S., Gobioff, H., Leung, S.: The Google file system. In: SOSP 2003: Proceedings of Nineteenth ACM SIGOPS Symposium on Operating Systems Principles. ACM Press (2003)
24. Google: Guava: Core Libraries for Java (2015). https://github.com/google/guava
25. Gupta, P., Zeldovich, N., Madden, S.: A trigger-based middleware cache for ORMs. In: Middleware (2011)
26. Holland, D.A., Angelino, E., Wald, G., Seltzer, M.I.: Flash caching on the storage client. In: USENIXATC (2013)
27. Java Community Process: JCACHE - Java Temporary Caching API (2014). https://jcp.org/en/jsr/detail?id=107

28. Johnson, T., Shasha, D.: 2Q: a low overhead high performance buffer management replacement algorithm. In: VLDB, pp. 439–450 (1994)
29. Kim, H., et al.: Flash-conscious cache population for enterprise database workloads. In: Fifth International Workshop on Accelerating Data Management Systems Using Modern Processor and Storage Architectures (2014)
30. Koller, R., Marmol, L., Rangaswami, R., Sundararaman, S., Talagala, N., Zhao, M.: Write policies for host-side Flash caches. In: FAST 2013 (2013)
31. Krüger, J., et al.: Fast updates on read-optimized databases using multi-core CPUs. PVLDB 5(1), 61–72 (2011)
32. Larson, P., Goldstein, J.J., Guo, H., Zhou, J.: MTCache: transparent mid-tier database caching in SQL server. In: ICDE (2004)
33. Megiddo, N., Modha, D.S.: ARC: a self-tuning, low overhead replacement cache. In: FAST. USENIX (2003)
34. Memcached. http://www.memcached.org/
35. Nishtala, R., et al.: Scaling Memcache at Facebook. In: NSDI, pp. 385–398. USENIX, Berkeley (2013)
36. O'Neil, E.J., O'Neil, P.E., Weikum, G.: The LRU-K page replacement algorithm for database disk buffering. In: ACM SIGMOD (1993)
37. Ports, D.R.K., Clements, A.T., Zhang, I., Madden, S., Liskov, B.: Transactional consistency and automatic management in an application data cache. In: OSDI. USENIX, October 2010
38. RedisLabs: Redis. https://redis.io/
39. Stonebraker, M.: Operating system support for database management. Commun. ACM 24(7), 412–418 (1981)
40. Stonebraker, M., Cattell, R.: 10 rules for scalable performance in simple operation datastores. Commun. ACM 54, 72–80 (2011)
41. Terracotta: BigMemory. http://terracotta.org/products/bigmemory
42. Voruganti, K., Özsu, M.T., Unrau, R.C.: An adaptive data-shipping architecture for client caching data management systems. Distrib. Parallel Databases 15(2), 137–177 (2004)
43. Whalin, G., Wang, X., Li, M.: Whalin Memcached Client Version 2.6.1. http://github.com/gwhalin/Memcached-Java-Client/releases/tag/release_2.6.1

Benchmarking and Performance Analysis of Event Sequence Queries on Relational Database

Yuto Hayamizu[1]([✉]) [iD], Ryoji Kawamichi[1], Kazuo Goda[1] [iD],
and Masaru Kitsuregawa[1,2] [iD]

[1] Institute of Industrial Science, The University of Tokyo, Tokyo, Japan
{haya,kawamichi,kgoda,kitsure}@tkl.iis.u-tokyo.ac.jp
[2] National Institute of Informatics, Tokyo, Japan

Abstract. The relational database has been the fundamental technology for data-driven decision making based on the histories of event occurrences about the analysis target. Thus the performance of analytical workloads in relational databases has been studied intensively. As a common language for performance analysis, decision support benchmarks such as TPC-H have been widely used. These benchmarks focus on summarization of the event occurrence information. Individual event occurrences or inter-occurrence associations are rarely examined in these benchmarks. However, this type of query, called an *event sequence query* in this paper, is becoming important in various real-world applications. Typically, an event sequence query extracts event sequences starting from a small number of interesting event occurrences. In a relational database, these queries are described by multiple self-joins on the whole sequence of events. Furthermore, each pair of events to be joined tends to have a strong correlation in the timestamp attribute, resulting in heavily skewed join workloads. Despite the usefulness in real-world data analysis, very little work has been done on performance analysis of event sequence queries.

In this paper, we present the initial design of ESQUE benchmark, a benchmark for event sequence queries. We then give experimental results of the comparison of database system implementations: PostgreSQL v.s. MySQL, and the comparison of historical versions of PostgreSQL. Conducted performance analysis shows that ESQUE benchmark allows us to discover performance problems which had been overlooked in existing benchmarks.

Keywords: Event sequence query · Relational database
Performance analysis · Benchmark · Data analytics

1 Introduction

The relational database has been the fundamental technology in decision support systems. The core of data-driven decision making is data analytics based

© Springer Nature Switzerland AG 2019
R. Nambiar and M. Poess (Eds.): TPCTC 2018, LNCS 11135, pp. 110–125, 2019.
https://doi.org/10.1007/978-3-030-11404-6_9

on the fact: the historical collection of event occurrences about analysis targets, e.g., histories of transactions, user activities on online services and health status changes of patients. The broader variety of event occurrences in the physical world is becoming digitally observable in the finer granularity more than ever [24]. It means that wider and deeper data analysis is becoming potentially feasible.

To fully utilize ever-increasing event occurrence data, performance improvement of data analytics has been identified as the most critical challenge to overcome. Thus, significant efforts have been devoted to performance studies of analytical query processing in relational database systems. In particular, several benchmarks for decision support systems were proposed as a foundation to conduct performance studies, e.g., TPC-H [20], TPC-DS [17], Star Schema Benchmark [19], and their derivatives [4, 18]. These benchmarks are designed to represent the typical workloads in the real-world analytics and widely accepted in both academia and industry. They are not only useful to compare transactions per second between multiple implementations, but also provide a common language for performance analysis. Benchmarks with well-defined data structures and workloads such as TPC-H gives the rigorous baseline of performance analysis. They have been empowering researchers and developers to find out performance problems and evaluating novel technologies.

In this paper, we shed light on an emerging type of workload which has been overlooked in conventional decision support benchmarks. The workloads of existing decision support benchmarks mainly focus on summarization of a large amount of event occurrence information stored in a single or the small number of fact tables. Individual event occurrences and inter-occurrence associations between event occurrences are rarely examined in these queries. For convenience, we named this type of query *event sequence query*. In various domains, an event sequence query is useful for analyzing rare cases. Here we present some example scenarios:

Scenario 1: medical episode analysis at a medical institution.
Querying patients who have the episode satisfying the following event sequence conditions: the patient diagnosed with CKD (chronic kidney disease), then underwent dialysis, then underwent kidney transplant surgery within a month, but again diagnosed with CKD within three months, and then underwent kidney transplant surgery again.

Scenario 2: influential early bird customer analysis at a digital game distributor.
Querying customers who have more than 10,000 video streaming subscribers and the purchase history satisfying the following event sequence conditions: for at least five game titles in the annual bestseller ranking, the customer purchased the title within a week of the release, then started video streaming of the title within a month, and the title ranked in the monthly bestsellers.

An event sequence query is expected to become more critical as more detailed event occurrence information is accumulated in relational databases. In a relational database, when an event occurrence is represented as a record in a fact table, subsequent event occurrences can be retrieved by applying a self-join to the fact table. We assume that relevant events are likely to occur in the near time; therefore, the timestamp of subsequent events tends to be strongly correlated, resulting in join workloads that are heavily skewed. Empirically event sequence queries are time-consuming; however, despite their usefulness in real-world data analysis, very little work has been done to analyze the performance of event sequence queries[1].

As a step toward performance analysis of event sequence queries, we propose ESQUE (**E**vent **S**equence **QUE**ry) benchmark. We describe the fundamental properties of event sequence queries on a relational database and present the initial design of ESQUE benchmark consisting of event sequence queries defined for the TPC-H dataset. We present experimental results with PostgreSQL and MySQL and point out performance problems that are overlooked by the well-established TPC-H benchmark.

The remainder of this paper is organized as follows. Section 2 describes the fundamental properties of event sequence queries. Section 3 presents the initial design of ESQUE benchmark. Section 4 presents the experimental results. Section 5 summarizes the related work, and Sect. 6 concludes this paper.

2   Event Sequence Queries on Relational Database

An event sequence queries is a subset of possible relational queries defined on a database schema which have tables with temporal attributes. While there is no clear semantic distinction between event sequence queries and other queries, we bravely first define the conditions of event sequence queries for the ease of discussion in the following sections.

2.1   Event Occurrence and Event Sequence

An *event occurrence* is a data composed of temporal information and some additional information about the event. A simple example of event occurrence is a record in `orders` table of TPC-H dataset. It has `o_orderdate` as temporal information and other attributes like `o_orderkey` and `o_custkey` as additional information about the order. A single record may represent multiple event occurrences. `lineitem` table in TPC-H dataset has three timestamp attributes `l_shipdate`, `l_commitdate` and `l_receiptdate`. They correspond to individual event occurrences. Temporal information of an event occurrence may be the point in time, a range in time, a set of ranges in time. Unless otherwise noted, we assume that an event occurrence e has one timestamp attribute denoted as $e.t$.

---

[1] Queries 25 and 29 defined in TPC-DS [17] join multiple relations recording event occurrences, but these queries do not clearly consider semantic relations between individual event occurrences.

When two event occurrences e_1, e_2 have a *connection*[2] described by a boolean value expression C, it is denoted as $e_1 \overset{\longleftrightarrow}{C} e_2$, and e_1, e_2 are *connected by C*. We assume that C must include a condition about a relationship between temporal information of e_1, e_2. Obvious examples of connection C is: $C = e_1.t < e_2.t$ (e_1 happens before e_2) and $C = e_1.t < e_2.t < e_1.t + L$ (e_2 happens within L after e_1 happens). When both $e_1 \overset{\longleftrightarrow}{C_1} e_2$ and $e_2 \overset{\longleftrightarrow}{C_2} e_3$ hold, e_2 and e_3 are also connected.

By collecting connected event occurrences starting from e_1, a finite set of event occurrences $(e_1, e_2, \cdots, e_n)$ is formed, and we call it an *event sequence*. An event sequence is also an event occurrence by regarding occurrences of $(e_1, e_2, \cdots, e_n)$ as a single event.

2.2 Event Sequence Queries in Relational Algebra

In the following discussion, we use the term an *event occurrence tuple* as a tuple corresponding to one event occurrence, and an *event occurrence relation* as a set of event occurrence tuples.

Here we define an *event sequence join operator* $\mathcal{T}_C$ as a particular form of join for event occurrence relations E_1, E_2, and an *event sequence query* as a relational query which includes at least one event sequence join operator.

$$E_1 \mathcal{T}_C E_2 \equiv \left\{ (e_1, e_2) \middle| e_1 \in E_1 \land e_2 \in E_2 \land e_1 \overset{\longleftrightarrow}{C} e_2 \right\} = \sigma_C(E_1 \times E_2)$$

Each resulting tuple of $E_1 \mathcal{T}_C E_2$ is an event sequence (a concatenated event tuples). Since an event sequence is also an event occurrence, $E_1 \mathcal{T}_C E_2$ is also an event occurrence relation, and we can recurse $\mathcal{T}_C$ operator like other relational algebra operators. $\mathcal{T}_C$ is interoperable with normal relational algebra operators as long as two operands of $\mathcal{T}_C$ are event occurrence relations.

2.3 Consideration on Workload Characteristics of Event Sequence Queries

Here we look back an example scenario of medical episode analysis described in Sect. 1: querying patients who have the episode satisfying the following event sequence conditions: the patient diagnosed with CKD, then underwent dialysis, then underwent kidney transplant surgery within a month, but again diagnosed with CKD within three months, and then underwent kidney transplant surgery again. Event sequence query of the example scenario should be defined on health log relation H like this:

---

[2] Although it might be better to call it a *relationship* between event occurrences, we use the term *connection* to avoid confusion with "relation" or "relational" in this paper.

$$_{\text{pid}}\mathcal{G}_{\text{distinct(pid)}}\left(\sigma_{\text{CKD}}(H) \underset{\substack{\text{after}\\\text{pid=pid}}}{\mathcal{T}} \sigma_{\text{dialysis}}(H) \underset{\substack{\text{within 1mon}\\\text{pid=pid}}}{\mathcal{T}} \sigma_{\text{surgery}}(H)\right.$$

$$\left.\underset{\substack{\text{within 3mon}\\\text{pid=pid}}}{\mathcal{T}} \sigma_{\text{CKD}}(H) \underset{\substack{\text{after}\\\text{pid=pid}}}{\mathcal{T}} \sigma_{\text{surgery}}(H)\right)$$

In our experiences, event sequence queries usually focus on interesting rare cases as shown in the example above. Thus selectivity of each selection from event occurrence relation is likely to be lower than 0.1–1% due to rarity of the analysis target and temporal proximity of each connected event occurrences. Assuming that such event sequence queries are typical cases, resulting workload would be highly selective scans and heavily skewed joins.

Efficiently handling skewed joins is known to be the difficult problem [4, 14]. Relational database systems often implement multiple algorithms for join, e.g., nested loop join, hash join, sort-merge join, and choose an algorithm which is estimated to be optimal based on statistics such as the number of records, data distribution of attributes, correlations between attributes, join productivity and so on. Therefore, estimating statistical information on join operations, in particular, the accuracy of estimating the cardinality of joins is known to affect query processing performance significantly [14, 15].

The two major causes of cardinality estimation error are (1) error amplification by multiple joins and (2) correlations between attributes in join conditions. Due to the nature of the join operation, cardinality estimation error is multiplied and amplified for each join operation. For example, in joins of five relations, if the cardinality estimation error in each combination is 20%, finally the error is amplified to 207%. Although there are many efforts on improving the precision of cardinality estimation in strong correlations [7], its effectiveness is still limited. In general, the stronger the correlation between connections is, the less accurate join cardinality estimation tends to be.

From the above discussion, it is not easy to efficiently execute event sequence queries, which consists of highly selective scans and many self-join operations. Despite the importance in many real-world applications, few performance studies on event sequence queries have been investigated, and at least there is no benchmark for event sequence queries.

3   The Initial Design of ESQUE Benchmark

In this section, we describe the design of ESQUE benchmark for a performance indicator of event sequence queries on a relational database.

Regarding generation of the dataset, we decided to adopt the TPC-H benchmark dataset for ESQUE benchmark instead of designing a dedicated dataset. We believe this strategy has benefits of usability and understandability of ESQUE benchmark for researchers and practitioners who are already familiar with TPC-H. The TPC-H dataset has a schema which imitates the database of wholesalers. It contains `orders` and `lineitem` tables, which can be regarded as event occurrence relations and is suitable for ESQUE benchmark.

Table 1. Queries in ESQUE benchmark (Relational algebraic expression describes only the outline of each query and full conditions are omitted. Please refer to SQL queries listed in the appendix for detail.)

ESQ.1	For each order in a specified month, retrieve a set of orders from the same customer in the month immediately following $$\pi\left(\sigma(\mathtt{O})\mathcal{T}\mathtt{L}\right)$$
ESQ.2	For specified customers, retrieve a set of parts that was bought by the customers over a specified period of three months and sold 100 or more within 3 months from the period $$\pi\left(\sigma(\mathtt{O}\bowtie\mathtt{L})\mathcal{T}\mathcal{G}(\sigma(\mathtt{O}\bowtie\mathtt{L}))\right)$$
ESQ.3	For orders made in specified six month period and includes a part "Brand #11", retrieve sequences of orders in which a customer making each initial order purchased a part "Brand #21" in next six months, and in which the same customer purchased a part "Brand#31" in the next six months $$\pi\left(\sigma(\mathtt{O}\bowtie\mathtt{L})\mathcal{T}\sigma(\mathtt{O}\bowtie\mathtt{L})\mathcal{T}\sigma(\mathtt{O}\bowtie\mathtt{L})\right)$$
ESQ.4	For each order within a specified month, retrieve the first five orders in which a given that the same customer purchased the same item $$\pi\left(\sigma(\mathtt{O}\bowtie\mathtt{L})\mathcal{T}\mathcal{G}(\sigma(\mathtt{O}\bowtie\mathtt{L}))\mathcal{T}\sigma(\mathtt{O}\bowtie\mathtt{L})\right)$$
ESQ.5	For a set of orders that was placed in a specified six month period, retrieve a set of orders that includes a part purchased within the specified six months and ordered within six months before the specified six months $$\pi\left(\mathcal{G}(\sigma(\mathtt{O}\bowtie\mathtt{L}))\mathcal{T}\sigma(\mathtt{O}\bowtie\mathtt{L})\right)$$
ESQ.6	For orders by specified customers, calculate the number of orders within a specified month, and retrieve the same number of orders within the immediately following month $$\sigma(\mathtt{O})\mathcal{T}\mathcal{G}(\sigma(\mathtt{O}))$$
ESQ.7	Within a specified fiscal year, find the day when the cumulative sales from the beginning of the fiscal year exceeded 1 million dollars $$\mathcal{G}\left(\mathcal{G}\left(\sigma(\mathtt{O})\right)\mathcal{T}\mathcal{G}(\sigma(\mathtt{O}))\right)$$

Based on the semantics of TPC-H dataset, we formed seven event sequence queries for the initial design of ESQUE benchmark. Table 1 lists assumed business questions and outlines of relational query representations. All queries start from an interesting initial set of orders such as orders by a small group of customers, orders within a specified period, orders including parts of specified brands, and a combination of these conditions, then retrieves event sequence.

As a first Because this is the first step of the performance study, we keep benchmark queries in relatively simple cases, at most three-event sequence joins.

Table 2. Experimental environment

Dell PowerEdge R740xd server	
Processor	x2 Intel Xeon Gold 6132 (14 cores, 28 threads)
Memory	96 GB (x12 8 GB 2,666 MHz DDR4 DIMM)
Storage (database)	RAID6 (22D+2P) w/PERC H740P Mini controller x24 Nearline-SAS 1.2TB 10Krpm HDDs
OS	CentOS 7.4 (Linux 3.10.0)

Table 3. Calibrated cost parameters in PostgreSQL

	PG 8.4	PG 9.2	PG 9.6	PG 10
seq_page_cost	1.70×10^{-3}	1.77×10^{-3}	2.27×10^{-3}	2.08×10^{-3}
random_page_cost	4.83	5.08	5.21	5.25
cpu_tuple_cost	5.63×10^{-5}	5.95×10^{-5}	6.25×10^{-5}	5.66×10^{-5}
cpu_operator_cost	1.09×10^{-4}	1.13×10^{-4}	6.68×10^{-5}	7.57×10^{-5}
cpu_index_tuple_cost	9.45×10^{-6}	1.29×10^{-5}	5.49×10^{-5}	4.90×10^{-5}

However, even for these simple queries, we discover that TPC-H benchmark overlooks several performance problems, which will be later reported in Sect. 4.

4   Experiments with ESQUE Benchmark

To evaluate the effectiveness of ESQUE benchmark as a performance index of event sequence queries, we conducted two experiments. The first experiment is performance comparison between different database system implementations: PostgreSQL v.s. MySQL and the second experiment is performance comparison between historical versions of PostgreSQL.

4.1   Experimental Setup

We ran all experiments on a server described in Table 2. For each version of PostgreSQL and MySQL (InnoDB), we created a 5TB ext4 partition on the RAID6 volume consisting of 24 Nearline-SAS HDDs and prepared a database by loading TPC-H dataset generated with scale factor = 1000 (1TB in raw).

In each version of PostgreSQL and MySQL, the size of the buffer pool[3] was set to 1 GB. We also configured parameters for cost estimation in query optimization. Configured parameters set the costs of primitive I/O and CPU operation in the cost estimation model of PostgreSQL's query optimizers. Because every component of PostgreSQL modules has been changed over time, execution

---

[3] shared_buffers(PostgreSQL) and innodb_buffer_pool_size(MySQL) were configured.

overheads of these primitive operations should be different between released versions of PostgreSQL. Regarding cost estimation accuracy, the best configuration for a certain version may not be the best one for other versions. Thus, we calibrated the costs of these operations separately for each version of PostgreSQL. We used the calibration methods presented by Hacigumus et al. [9] to determine parameter values because it was shown to give good estimates of the costs of query execution plans in TPC-H queries. Configured parameters and calibration results for each version are listed in Table 3.

In all experiments presented in this paper, we measured query execution time under the cold start condition; on each measurement, the cache memory of storage controller and the page cache of the Linux kernel were cleared, and the server process of a database system was restarted.

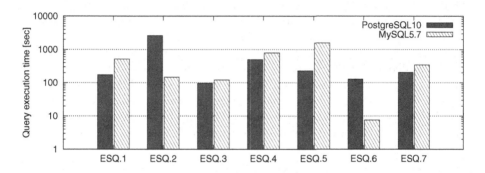

Fig. 1. Query execution time of ESQUE benchmark queries

4.2 Performance Comparison Between PostgreSQL and MySQL

We conducted performance measurements of ESQUE benchmark queries with PostgreSQL10.0 and MySQL5.7 and examined the performance characteristics of them.

Figure 1 shows query execution time of ESQUE benchmark queries. Note that the vertical axis is in logarithmic scale.

The result shows that PostgreSQL was faster than MySQL in five of the seven queries, ESQ.1, ESQ.3, ESQ.4, ESQ.5 and ESQ.7, and PostgreSQL was 16.6 times or slower than MySQL for ESQ.2 and ESQ.6. These performance differences come from the fact that MySQL used only nested loop joins and index scans while PostgreSQL also used hash joins, parallel sequential scans and bitmap index scans[4] in several parts of query plans.

---

[4] PostgreSQL's bitmap index scan is a search algorithm on B^+-tree and not an index data structure using bitmaps. In PostgreSQL implementation, bitmap index scan fetches only record pointers from B^+-tree indices, sorts record pointers by block address, and then fetches records from a table.

For ESQ.1, ESQ.3, ESQ.4, ESQ.5 and ESQ.7, PostgreSQL used hash joins, parallel sequential scans and bitmap index scans as part of query execution plans. They effectively improved storage access sequentiality of query execution plans compared to plans with only nested loop joins and index scans and resulted in better performance than MySQL.

For ESQ.2, PostgreSQL selected a query execution plan with a hash join which built a hash table from the whole `lineitem` table, which resulted in significant I/O footprint and longer execution time than MySQL. For ESQ.6, PostgreSQL was 16.6 times slower than MySQL because PostgreSQL used a multi-index bitmap index scan[5] instead of a single index scan for the correlated subquery, which repeats about 27,000 times. It incurred much more CPU overhead than a single index scan due to the computation of intersections. While the multi-index bitmap index scan can reduce the number of table page accesses per subquery execution, the most of page accessed were already cached in the buffer pool by previous executions of the subquery, and the I/O footprint reduction had little impact on total query execution time in ESQ.2.

For the richer implementations of access paths and join algorithms, PostgreSQL has considered being faster than MySQL regarding TPC-H or decision support queries [2,23]. On the contrary to common sense, ESQUE benchmark revealed that there exist some event sequence queries in which PostgreSQL is slower than MySQL at most 16.6 times. These results indicate the effectiveness of ESQUE benchmark as a performance indicator for database system comparison.

4.3   Performance Comparison Between PostgreSQL Versions

In this experiment, we compared the performance of historical versions of PostgreSQL releases: 8.4, 9.2, 9.6, 10.0 with TPC-H benchmark and ESQUE benchmark. Figure 2(a) shows the result with TPC-H[6] and Fig. 2(b) shows the result with ESQUE benchmark. In each figure, the horizontal axis represents the version number of PostgreSQL, and the vertical axis represents relative query execution time normalized by query execution time of PostgreSQL 8.4 for each query. Note that the vertical axis is in logarithmic scale. When a curve of a query goes below 1.0 as the version number increase, it means that performance is improved regarding the query.

As clearly depicted in Fig. 2(a), all of the TPC-H queries except Q.9 ran faster in PostgreSQL10.0 than in PostgreSQL8.4. TPC-H benchmark is the well-established performance indicator. This result presumably indicates that TPC-H

---

[5] When multiple B^{+}-tree indexes are available on the single table, PostgreSQL's optimizer may choose a query execution plan using bitmap index scan on multiple B^{+}-tree indexes. We call it *multi-index bitmap index scan*. A multi-index bitmap scan first searches multiple B^{+}-tree indexes and compute the intersection of record pointers, and then fetches the records.

[6] We omitted TPC-H Q.4, Q.20, and Q.21 from the measurement of this experiment because these queries did not finish in 24 h for PostgreSQL 8.4 and 9.2.

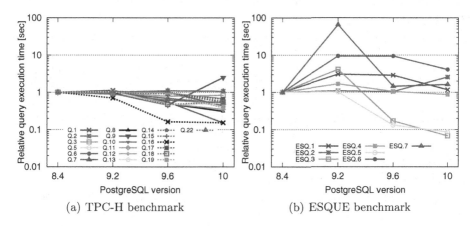

Fig. 2. Historical performance trends of PostgreSQL in TPC-H benchmark and ESQUE benchmark

performance has been continuously checked and feedbacked to the development of PostgreSQL.

Performance degradation of Q.9 at PostgreSQL10.0 is caused by the use of parallel sequential scan[7]. In PostgreSQL, worker processes of parallel sequential scan share single scan pointer on a table file and each page fetch operation are serialized. Therefore, parallel sequential scan tends to be slower than normal sequential scan due to synchronization overhead for heavily I/O intensive scan workloads.

On the contrary to TPC-H benchmark, query execution time of ESQUE queries fluctuated up to 65 times longer over historical versions. Four of seven queries ran slower in PostgreSQL10.0 than in PostgreSQL8.4 as depicted in Fig. 2(b). By analyzing the measurement results and source code of PostgreSQL, we found that these performance degradations are caused by following reasons:

1. Overestimated cost of evaluating an expression consisting of many AND-ed expressions
2. Underestimated cost of repeated subqueries consisting of multi-index bitmap index scans (described in Sect. 4.3)
3. The change of the cost estimation logic introduced at PostgreSQL10.0.

As far as we confirmed throughout our experiments, TPC-H benchmark could not detect performance degradation caused by all three reasons. This result supports the effectiveness of ESQUE benchmark as a performance indicator of database system development. We have already submitted a patch to PostgreSQL community for the reason 1, and currently working on patches for the reason 2 and 3.

---

[7] Parallel sequential scan was first introduced at PostgreSQL9.6, but it was not selected for any queries by query optimizer of PostgreSQL9.6 in this experiment.

5   Related Work

Benchmarking have been the fundamental of the evolution of database systems both academically and commercially. As stated by Boncz et al. [5], a good benchmark not only allows practitioners to evaluate different technologies quantitatively but also stimulates technological advancements. For analytical processing on a relational database, benchmarks for decision support systems have been intensively investigated. TPC-H [20] is the most widely used benchmark in both academia and industry, and there also exists several prominent benchmarks such as TPC-DS [17] and Star Schema Benchmark [18]. Queries 25 and 29 defined in TPC-DS [17] join multiple relations recording event occurrences, but these queries do not clearly consider semantic relations between individual event occurrences. Nambiar et al. presented an approach for generating synthetic sequence database for benchmarking [16]. However, performance studies or benchmarks of event sequence queries have not been studied as far as we know in the literature, despite its importance in various application domains, e.g., health care.

Event information stored in a database can be regarded as a kind of time-series data. The common approach for analyzing time-series is pattern mining. Early work on pattern mining had been discussed in the field of artificial intelligence [8]. As initial research on pattern mining in the field of database research, Agrawal et al. proposed several pattern mining algorithms for extracting periodic patterns from transaction histories [1], and there followed a wide variety of work, e.g., pattern mining algorithms for partially periodic patterns [10], efficiency improvements of pattern mining algorithms [3,11], application-oriented mining techniques [29]. Pattern mining is a technique for discovering frequent patterns of events and technically orthogonal to event sequence queries for retrieving individual events of interest.

Regarding data retrieval from time series data, similar pattern search in numerical data sequence like stock chart histories have been studied. As a pioneering work, Faloutsos et al. proposed the approach to use R*-tree for similar pattern search by mapping a slice of data series to a point in a high dimensional feature space. Jagadish et al. showed that Dynamic Time Warping (DTW) is better than Euclidean distance for indexing in a feature space [30]. Keogh et al. proposed a method of efficiently exact match retrieval using DTW [12]. There are also studies such as compression of a feature space by Fourier transform [6], its extension and generalization [21]. The target of similar pattern search is the search based on the pattern of the numerical time-series data, while the target of event sequence queries discussed in this paper is not limited to the numerical time-series data.

There are also efforts to extend the data model and query description language to make the handling of time-series data more efficient or to make it easier in a relational database. Seshadri et al. proposed a data model SEQ, an extension of the relational model for sequence data [26], and also showed query optimization techniques in SEQ [27]. As a proposal to extend SQL for time-series data applications, there exist several proposals, e.g., SRQL [22] by Ramakrishnan et al. SQL-TS [25] by Sadri et al. TSQL2 [28] by Snodgrass, extended by streaming data by Law et al. [13].

6 Conclusion

In this paper, we pointed out the importance of performance analysis of event sequence queries in a relational database and presented an initial design of ESQUE benchmark for the foundation of performance analysis of event sequence queries. By conducting experiments with PostgreSQL and MySQL on 1TB TPC-H dataset, we found multiple performance problems which cannot be detected by well-established TPC-H benchmark and have been overlooked for years.

The presented design of ESQUE benchmark is just a first step and still limited to example-based query definitions. In future work, we would like to make ESQUE benchmark covering representative workloads of event sequence queries more extensively, and evaluate its effectiveness with experiments in the broader variety of database system implementations.

Acknowledgment. This paper is in part based on results obtained from a project commissioned by the New Energy and Industrial Technology Development Organization (NEDO).

Appendix. SQL Queries in ESQUE Benchmark

ESQ.1

```
SELECT e.o_orderkey, e.o_custkey, date_trunc('month', e.o_orderdate),
  f.o_orderkey, f.o_custkey, date_trunc('month', f.o_orderdate)
FROM orders e, orders f
WHERE e.o_custkey = f.o_custkey
  AND f.o_orderdate
    BETWEEN date_trunc('month', e.o_orderdate) + INTERVAL '[MONTHS] month'
    AND date_trunc('month', e.o_orderdate)
      + interval '[MONTHS] month' * 2 - INTERVAL '1 day'
  AND e.o_orderdate BETWEEN CAST('[DATE]' AS date)
    AND CAST('[DATE]' AS date) + INTERVAL '[MONTHS] month' - INTERVAL '1 day'
  AND e.o_custkey BETWEEN 1 AND [CUSTKEY];
```

Default values: [MONTHS] = 3, [CUSTKEY] = 10000, [DATE] = 1994-1-1

ESQ.2

```
SELECT e_orderkey, e_partkey,
  e_orderdate + f_info[1] * interval '1 day' as f_min_orderdate,
  e_orderdate + f_info[2] * interval '1 day' as f_max_orderdate,
  f_info[3] AS f_quantity, f_info[4] AS f_order_count
FROM
  (SELECT e.o_orderkey as e_orderkey, e.l_partkey as e_partkey,
    e.o_orderdate as e_orderdate,
    (SELECT ARRAY[min(o_orderdate) - e.o_orderdate,
              max(o_orderdate) - e.o_orderdate,
              sum(l_quantity), count(*)]
     FROM orders fo INNER JOIN lineitem fl ON o_orderkey = l_orderkey
```

```
    WHERE fo.o_orderdate BETWEEN e.o_orderdate + INTERVAL '1 day'
                        AND e.o_orderdate + INTERVAL '[MONTH] month'
      AND fl.l_partkey = e.l_partkey
    GROUP BY fl.l_partkey) as f_info
  FROM
    (SELECT * FROM orders INNER JOIN lineitem ON o_orderkey = l_orderkey
    WHERE o_orderdate BETWEEN cast('[DATE]' AS date)
                      AND CAST('[DATE]' as date)
                              + INTERVAL '[MONTH] month' - INTERVAL '1 day'
      AND o_custkey BETWEEN 1 AND [CUSTKEY]) e) AS result WHERE f_info[3] > 100;
```

Default values: [MONTHS] = 3, [CUSTKEY] = 150, [DATE] = 1994-1-1

ESQ.3

```
SELECT e.o_orderkey, e.o_orderdate, e.o_custkey,
  e.l_partkey, f.o_orderkey, f.o_orderdate,
  f.l_partkey, g.o_orderkey, g.o_orderdate, g.l_partkey
FROM
  (SELECT * FROM orders
   INNER JOIN lineitem on o_orderkey = l_orderkey
   INNER JOIN part ON l_partkey = p_partkey
                  AND p_brand = '[BRAND1]') e,
  (SELECT * FROM orders
   INNER JOIN lineitem on o_orderkey = l_orderkey
   INNER JOIN part ON l_partkey = p_partkey
                  AND p_brand = '[BRAND2]') f,
  (SELECT * FROM orders
   INNER JOIN lineitem on o_orderkey = l_orderkey
   INNER JOIN part ON l_partkey = p_partkey
                  AND p_brand = '[BRAND3]') g
WHERE f.o_custkey = e.o_custkey AND g.o_custkey = e.o_custkey
  AND e.o_custkey BETWEEN 1 and [CUSTKEY]
  AND f.o_orderdate BETWEEN (e.o_orderdate + 1)
    AND (e.o_orderdate + interval '[MONTH] month')
  AND g.o_orderdate BETWEEN (f.o_orderdate + 1)
    AND (e.o_orderdate + interval '[MONTH] month' * 2)
  AND e.o_orderdate BETWEEN CAST('[DATE]' AS date)
    AND CAST('[DATE]' AS date) +
  INTERVAL '[MONTH] month' - INTERVAL '1 day';
```

Default values: [MONTHS] = 6, [CUSTKEY] = 1000, [DATE] = 1994-1-1, [BRAND1]
= Brand#11, [BRAND2] = Brand#21, [BRAND3] = Brand#31

ESQ.4

```
SELECT e.o_orderkey, e.o_orderdate, e.o_custkey,
  e.p_brand, f.o_orderkey, f.o_orderdate, f.o_custkey, f.p_brand
FROM
  (SELECT * FROM orders INNER JOIN lineitem
    ON o_orderkey = l_orderkey INNER JOIN part
    ON l_partkey = p_partkey) e,
  (SELECT * FROM orders INNER JOIN lineitem
    ON o_orderkey = l_orderkey INNER JOIN part
    ON l_partkey = p_partkey) f
WHERE f.o_custkey = e.o_custkey AND f.p_brand = e.p_brand
  AND e.o_custkey BETWEEN 1 AND [CUSTKEY] AND f.o_custkey BETWEEN 1 AND [CUSTKEY]
  AND (SELECT count(*) FROM orders
        WHERE o_custkey = e.o_custkey
        AND o_orderdate BETWEEN (e.o_orderdate + INTERVAL '1 day')
          AND f.o_orderdate
        AND o_custkey BETWEEN 1 AND [CUSTKEY]) BETWEEN 1 and 5
  AND e.o_orderdate BETWEEN CAST('[DATE]' AS date)
    AND cast('[DATE]' AS date) + INTERVAL '[MONTHS] month' - INTERVAL '1 day';
```

Default values: [MONTHS] = 1, [CUSTKEY] = 10000, [DATE] = 1994-1-1

ESQ.5

```
SELECT f.l_partkey, f.o_orderkey, f.o_orderdate
FROM (SELECT distinct l_partkey
        FROM orders INNER JOIN lineitem ON o_orderkey = l_orderkey
        WHERE o_orderdate BETWEEN CAST('[DATE]' as DATE)
          AND CAST('[DATE]' AS date) + INTERVAL '[MONTH] month'
          - INTERVAL '1 day' AND o_custkey BETWEEN 1 AND [CUSTKEY]) e
INNER JOIN
  (SELECT l_partkey, o_orderkey, o_orderdate
    FROM orders INNER JOIN lineitem ON o_orderkey = l_orderkey
    WHERE o_orderdate BETWEEN CAST('[DATE]' AS date)
      - INTERVAL '[month] month'
      AND CAST('[DATE]' AS DATE) - INTERVAL '1 day'
    AND o_custkey BETWEEN 1 AND [CUSTKEY]) f
ON e.l_partkey = f.l_partkey
```

Default values: [MONTHS] = 1, [CUSTKEY] = 25000, [DATE] = 1994-1-1

ESQ.6

```
SELECT * FROM orders fo
WHERE fo.o_orderdate >= CAST('[DATE]' as date)
  + INTERVAL '[MONTHS] month' + INTERVAL '1 day'
  AND fo.o_custkey BETWEEN 1 AND [CUSTKEY]
  AND (SELECT count(*) FROM orders co
        WHERE co.o_orderdate BETWEEN
          CAST('[DATE]' AS date) + INTERVAL '[MONTHS] month'
          + INTERVAL '1 day' AND fo.o_orderdate
        and o_custkey BETWEEN 1 AND [CUSTKEY])
  < (SELECT count(eo.*)
      FROM orders eo
      WHERE o_orderdate BETWEEN CAST('[DATE]' AS date)
      AND CAST('[DATE]' AS date) + INTERVAL '[MONTHS] month'
      - INTERVAL '1 day' AND o_custkey BETWEEN 1 and [CUSTKEY]);
```

Default values: [MONTHS] = 1, [CUSTKEY] = 500, [DATE] = 1994-1-1

ESQ.7

```
SELECT min(o_orderdate) FROM (
 SELECT e.o_orderdate FROM
  (SELECT distinct o_orderdate
   FROM orders
   WHERE o_orderdate
     BETWEEN CAST('[DATE]' as date)
       AND CAST('[DATE]' as date) + INTERVAL '[MONTHS] month'
   AND o_custkey between 1 and [CUSTKEY]) e
 WHERE
  (SELECT sum(o_totalprice) FROM orders
   WHERE o_orderdate
     BETWEEN CAST('[DATE]' as date)
       AND CAST('[DATE]' as date) + INTERVAL '[MONTHS] month'
   AND o_orderdate <= e.o_orderdate
   AND o_custkey BETWEEN 1 AND [CUSTKEY]) >=1000000
) a;
```

Default values: [MONTHS] = 1, [CUSTKEY] = 6000, [DATE] = 1994-1-1

References

1. Agrawal, R., Srikant, R.: Mining sequential patterns. In: Proceedings of the Eleventh International Conference on Data Engineering, ICDE 1995, pp. 3–14. IEEE Computer Society, Washington, DC (1995)
2. Alagiannis, I., Borovica, R., Branco, M., Idreos, S., Ailamaki, A.: NoDB: efficient query execution on raw data files. In: Proceedings of the 2012 ACM SIGMOD International Conference on Management of Data, SIGMOD 2012, pp. 241–252. ACM, New York (2012)
3. Ayres, J., Flannick, J., Gehrke, J., Yiu, T.: Sequential PAttern mining using a bitmap representation. In: Proceedings of the Eighth ACM SIGKDD International Conference on Knowledge Discovery and Data Mining, KDD 2002, pp. 429–435. ACM, New York (2002)
4. Boncz, P., Anatiotis, A.-C., Kläbe, S.: JCC-H: adding join crossing correlations with skew to TPC-H. In: Nambiar, R., Poess, M. (eds.) TPCTC 2017. LNCS, vol. 10661, pp. 103–119. Springer, Cham (2018). https://doi.org/10.1007/978-3-319-72401-0_8
5. Boncz, P., Neumann, T., Erling, O.: TPC-H analyzed: hidden messages and lessons learned from an influential benchmark. In: Nambiar, R., Poess, M. (eds.) TPCTC 2013. LNCS, vol. 8391, pp. 61–76. Springer, Cham (2014). https://doi.org/10.1007/978-3-319-04936-6_5
6. Chan, K.P., Fu, A.W.C.: Efficient time series matching by wavelets. In: Proceedings 15th International Conference on Data Engineering (Cat. No. 99CB36337), pp. 126–133, March 1999
7. Chaudhuri, S.: An overview of query optimization in relational systems. In: Proceedings of the Seventeenth ACM SIGACT-SIGMOD-SIGART Symposium on Principles of Database Systems, PODS 1998, pp. 34–43. ACM, New York (1998)
8. Dietterich, T.G., Michalski, R.S.: Discovering patterns in sequences of events. Artif. Intell. **25**(2), 187–232 (1985)
9. Hacigumus, H., Chi, Y., Wu, W., Zhu, S., Tatemura, J., Naughton, J.F.: Predicting query execution time: are optimizer cost models really unusable? In: Proceedings of the 2013 IEEE International Conference on Data Engineering (ICDE 2013), ICDE 2013, pp. 1081–1092. IEEE Computer Society, Washington, DC (2013)
10. Han, J., Dong, G., Yin, Y.: Efficient mining of partial periodic patterns in time series database. In: Proceedings 15th International Conference on Data Engineering (Cat. No. 99CB36337), pp. 106–115, March 1999
11. Han, J., Pei, J., Mortazavi-Asl, B., Chen, Q., Dayal, U., Hsu, M.C.: FreeSpan: frequent pattern-projected sequential pattern mining. In: Proceedings of the Sixth ACM SIGKDD International Conference on Knowledge Discovery and Data Mining, KDD 2000, pp. 355–359. ACM, New York (2000)
12. Keogh, E.: Exact indexing of dynamic time warping. In: Proceedings of the 28th International Conference on Very Large Data Bases, VLDB 2002, pp. 406–417. VLDB Endowment (2002)
13. Law, Y.N., Wang, H., Zaniolo, C.: Query languages and data models for database sequences and data streams. In: Proceedings of the Thirtieth International Conference on Very Large Data Bases - Volume 30, VLDB 2004, pp. 492–503. VLDB Endowment (2004)
14. Leis, V., Gubichev, A., Mirchev, A., Boncz, P., Kemper, A., Neumann, T.: How good are query optimizers, really? Proc. VLDB Endow. **9**(3), 204–215 (2015)

15. Moerkotte, G., Neumann, T., Steidl, G.: Preventing bad plans by bounding the impact of cardinality estimation errors. Proc. VLDB Endow. **2**(1), 982–993 (2009)
16. Moussa, R.: *Big-SeqDB-Gen*: a formal and scalable approach for parallel generation of big synthetic sequence databases. In: Nambiar, R., Poess, M. (eds.) TPCTC 2015. LNCS, vol. 9508, pp. 61–76. Springer, Cham (2016). https://doi.org/10.1007/978-3-319-31409-9_5
17. Nambiar, R.O., Poess, M.: The making of TPC-DS. In: Proceedings of the 32nd International Conference on Very Large Data Bases, VLDB 2006, pp. 1049–1058. VLDB Endowment (2006)
18. O'Neil, P., O'Neil, E., Chen, X., Revilak, S.: The star schema benchmark and augmented fact table indexing. In: Nambiar, R., Poess, M. (eds.) TPCTC 2009. LNCS, vol. 5895, pp. 237–252. Springer, Heidelberg (2009). https://doi.org/10.1007/978-3-642-10424-4_17
19. O'Neil, P.E., O'Neil, E.J., Chen, X.: The star schema benchmark (SSB). Pat **200**, 50 (2007)
20. Poess, M., Floyd, C.: New TPC benchmarks for decision support and web commerce. SIGMOD Rec. **29**(4), 64–71 (2000)
21. Rafiei, D., Mendelzon, A.O.: Querying time series data based on similarity. IEEE Trans. Knowl. Data Eng. **12**(5), 675–693 (2000)
22. Ramakrsihnan, R., Donjerkovic, D., Ranganathan, A., Beyer, K.S., Krishnaprasad, M.: SRQL: sorted relational query language. In: Proceedings of Tenth International Conference on Scientific and Statistical Database Management (Cat. No. 98TB100243), pp. 84–95, July 1998
23. Ray, S., Simion, B., Brown, A.D.: Jackpine: a benchmark to evaluate spatial database performance. In: 2011 IEEE 27th International Conference on Data Engineering, pp. 1139–1150, April 2011
24. Reinsel, D., Gantz, J., Rydning, J.: Data Age 2025: The Evolution of Data to Life-Critical. Don't Focus on Big Data (2017)
25. Sadri, R., Zaniolo, C., Zarkesh, A., Adibi, J.: Optimization of sequence queries in database systems. In: Proceedings of the Twentieth ACM SIGMOD-SIGACT-SIGART Symposium on Principles of Database Systems, PODS 2001, pp. 71–81. ACM, New York (2001)
26. Seshadri, P., Livny, M., Ramakrishnan, R.: SEQ: a model for sequence databases. In: Proceedings of the Eleventh International Conference on Data Engineering, pp. 232–239, March 1995
27. Seshadri, P., Livny, M., Ramakrishnan, R.: Sequence query processing. In: Proceedings of the 1994 ACM SIGMOD International Conference on Management of Data, SIGMOD 1994, pp. 430–441. ACM, New York (1994)
28. Snodgrass, R.: The TSQL2 Temporal Query Language. The Springer International Series in Engineering and Computer Science. Springer, New York (2012). https://doi.org/10.1007/978-1-4615-2289-8
29. Srivastava, J., Cooley, R., Deshpande, M., Tan, P.N.: Web usage mining: discovery and applications of usage patterns from web data. SIGKDD Explor. Newsl. **1**(2), 12–23 (2000)
30. Yi, B.K., Jagadish, H.V., Faloutsos, C.: Efficient retrieval of similar time sequences under time warping. In: Proceedings 14th International Conference on Data Engineering, pp. 201–208, February 1998

Data Consistency Properties
of Document Store as a Service (DSaaS):
Using MongoDB Atlas as an Example

Chenhao Huang[1]([✉]), Michael Cahill[2], Alan Fekete[1], and Uwe Röhm[1]

[1] School of Information Technologies, University of Sydney, Sydney, Australia
{chenhao.huang,alan.fekete,uwe.roehm}@sydney.edu.au
[2] MongoDB Inc., Sydney, Australia
michael.cahill@mongodb.com

Abstract. Document-oriented database systems, also known as document stores, are attractive for building modern web applications where the speed of development and deployment are critical, especially due to the prevalence of data in document-structured formats such as JSON and XML. MongoDB Atlas is a hosted offering of MongoDB as a Service, which is easy to set up, operate, and scale in the cloud. Like many NoSQL stores, MongoDB Atlas allows users to accept possible temporary inconsistency among the replicas, as a trade-off for lower latency and higher availability during partitions. In this work, we describe an empirical study to quantify the amount of inconsistency observed in data that is held in MongoDB Atlas.

Keywords: Document Storage as a Service (DSaaS)
Consistency benchmarking · NoSQL

1 Introduction

A variety of Document Storage as a Service (DSaaS) systems have become quite popular in recent years. They provide an easy growth and pay-as-you-go choice to the developers, who want to use a document store for their data management and to run in a public cloud environment.

There are two characteristics of Document Storage as a Service (DSaaS). Firstly, they are document store, which means they support a semistructured data model based on hierarchical documents, often expressed with JSON. This is useful in web application development. Secondly, they are hosted, as a service, that is the management of the data is not owned by the organization with the data. Nowadays, cloud customers have a wide range of options if they would like to use a document store: they can either use an integrated service provided by the cloud owner, such as Microsoft Azure DocumentDB [18], or use the service provided by a third party, such as MongoDB Atlas[1].

---

[1] https://www.mongodb.com/cloud/atlas/.

© Springer Nature Switzerland AG 2019
R. Nambiar and M. Poess (Eds.): TPCTC 2018, LNCS 11135, pp. 126–139, 2019.
https://doi.org/10.1007/978-3-030-11404-6_10

MongoDB Atlas is a "containerized" version of existing MongoDB. MongoDB Atlas has the same core as the open source Community Server, but with some additional, closed source code functionality (e.g., security features). The lower tiers (M0, M2 and M5) have a layer added on top of standalone MongoDB for multi-tenant support. Customers are able to use the MongoDB Atlas in a pay-as-you-go model, hosted on diverse cloud service platforms: Amazon Web Service (AWS), Microsoft Azure, or Google Cloud Platform. They can also select the service locations, memory and storage size, number of CPUs, etc. The database can be deployed with a few clicks and around 10 min waiting. It is also trivial to scale-up if more computational power or storage are needed. Moreover, MongoDB Atlas has various APIs for different programming languages and applications.

Like many NoSQL data storage systems, MongoDB Atlas typically splits large files into blocks. It replicates the blocks, places replicas in different nodes, and balances work among the nodes. This offers many advantages, including using low-cost commercial hardware, tolerance to network and hardware failures, etc. However, in this case, perfect data consistency will be sacrificed in order to tolerate partitions and keep the latency low, as described by the CAP theorem [12] and PACELC formulation [4]. Several recent works such as [7,9,19] have attempted to give a quantitative measure to the amount of inconsistency that arises in execution of a NoSQL store, to help developers understand more clearly how much risk applies to correctness of the systems they are building. So far, this research has concentrated on key-value stores, especially those whose design is based on that of Dynamo [13]. In this paper we seek to achieve the same kind of measurement of data inconsistency for MongoDB Atlas.

The metric that we use to describe the consistency property of a store, is the probability that a read will see a *stale* value (that is, a value that is different from what was installed by the latest write). This probability varies, depending on the time elapsed between the last write, and the read concerned. In 2010, on Amazon SimpleDB, staleness probabilities up to 66% were observed, for an extended period lasting up to 500 ms [19], suggesting that 2 out of 3 replicas were not seeing a write for quite a while. When attempting to now do a similar measurement on MongoDB Atlas, we found quite different properties, and these in fact required some adjustments to the measurement approach. The contributions of our paper are the description of how we benchmarked the consistency level of MongoDB Atlas, the results we obtained, and the insights we draw from those.

The paper is structured as follows. Section 2 briefly introduces MongoDB and MongoDB Atlas, and explains the replication protocol of these systems. Section 3 explains our benchmarking method. The benchmarking results are recorded in Sect. 4, with a few different configurations of read preference, as well as the analysis of the operation latency. In Sect. 5.2, we consider how we had to vary the measurement details from the original model from [19]. Section 6 describes the related work and in Sect. 7 is a summary of the paper.

2   MongoDB Atlas

As mentioned in Sect. 1, MongoDB Atlas is a hosted MongoDB as a Service provided by MongoDB. Customers only have the freedom for a limited number of configurations, for instance, the cloud service platforms, service regions, memory and storage size, the number of vCPUs, etc. This hosted MongoDB service is very convenient for the end users.

MongoDB Atlas uses the default MongoDB architecture - one primary copy and a few secondary copies. All write requests are sent to the primary copy first, and then the written value propagates to all secondary copies later on. The propagation mechanism is an internal setting and is not visible to the users. However, the consumers can decide when MongoDB considers the writes are successful and acknowledges the driver in *write concerns*. Concretely, the users can specify a number, or simply put the key word "majority", in the *write concerns* [2]. In this case, the MongoDB waits until *that* number of replicas (or a "majority" of replicas) reply, before it responds to the driver. Here is an example. Suppose our MongoDB cluster has three nodes (Fig. 1). If the default setting of the *write concern* is selected, then the writes are considered successful once the primary copy replies (shown in Fig. 1(A)). Otherwise, if you choose a certain number n for the *write concerns*, the MongoDB waits until n writes confirm (shown in Fig. 1(B) and (C)), before sending a response to the driver. In Fig. 1(B), the *write concern* is 2; while in Fig. 1(C), the *write concern* is 3.

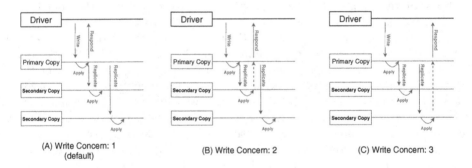

(A) Write Concern: 1 (default)   (B) Write Concern: 2   (C) Write Concern: 3

Fig. 1. The behavior of MongoDB with different *write concern* settings   (Figure adapted from [3])

On the other hand, MongoDB also allows you to choose *read preference*. *Read preference* describes which replica(s) MongoDB clients send reading requests to. There are five *read preferences*, including *primary* (default), *primaryPreferred*, *secondary*, *secondaryPreferred*, and *nearest* [1]. If the read preference *primary* or *secondary* is selected, all read requests are only sent to the primary replica or one of the secondary members (shown in Fig. 2(A) and (B)). *PrimaryPreferred* and *secondaryPreferred* provide the users options that most of reads go to primary or secondary copy, however, in the situation where the preferred replica is not available, the driver sends the read request to other members. The read preference *nearest* is designed so that operation reads from the replica with the least network latency (shown in Fig. 2(C)). Here are some common use case for using non-primary read preference: (a) The running systems have no impact on the frond end applications; (b) When the MongoDB instance is geographically distributed, non-primary read preference can be used to provide low latency; (c) When there is a fail-over, non-primary read preference is able to maintain availability.

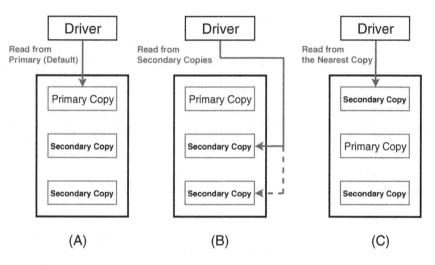

Fig. 2. The behavior of MongoDB client with different *read preferences* settings (Figure adapted from [1])

In our work, we benchmark three different read preferences: *primary* (default), *secondary*, and the *nearest*.

3   Benchmarking Consistency of MongoDB Atlas

In this section, we present and analyze the client-centric benchmarking approach used in our work. In general, we treat MongoDB Atlas as a "black box", neglecting the internal settings and configurations. This is exactly what a customer would experience in the real world. The benchmarking method follows that of Wada [19].

In this section, we introduce the benchmarking methods first, and then provide the implementation details, including the MongoDB Atlas cluster we benchmark and the AWS instance we use to run our benchmarking application.

3.1   Benchmarking Methods

There are three roles in our benchmarking application: one reader, one writer, and one MongoDB Atlas cluster (shown in Fig. 3). The writer repeatedly writes the current time stamp (in Nanoseconds) into a data element in the MongoDB Atlas cluster once every three seconds. The reader continuously reads from the same data element as fast as possible. The reader and the writer are kept in separate processes. A log is kept with entries for the start time of each operation, and later, the time when the operation returns (and, also the return value, for a read this is the value observed in the item). An analysis script (written in Java) processes the log after the experiments, detecting cases where a read saw a stale value. During the data analysis phase, we only look at those reads where, when the reading request is sent out, the writing request before it has already acknowledged (shown in Fig. 7(B)). The reasons for this exclusion can be found in Sect. 5.2.

After analysis we produce a report which shows, for a given time t, the probability of a read seeing a stale value, among all the reads which are submitted approximately t later than the previous write. To be precise, we form a bucket which contains all reads whose delay from the previous write is in the interval from t ms to $(t + 1)$ ms, and consider the ratio, among the reads in this bucket, of the number that retrieved a stale value, to the total number of reads in the bucket. We also look at the distribution among all operations of a kind (read or write), of the time elapsed from the request till the response. This is the latency of the operation.

We refer to one "measurement" of the experiment as running 50,000 reads and 29 writes. Each "measurement" has a 200-s window to run, while the actual time needed for each "measurement" in less than 100 s. This means that the system rests for around 100 s between two "measurements".

We run our benchmarking application for around 5,000 "measurements" during April, May, and June in 2018. The total running time is more than twelve days.

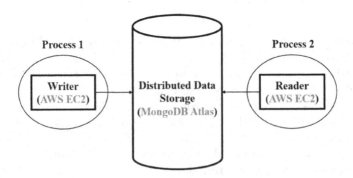

Fig. 3. The architecture of the benchmarking application. Note that the writer and the reader are in the same EC2 instance.

3.2 Implementation

MongoDB Atlas is a Document Storage as a Service (DSaaS) provided by MongoDB, and it is the main subject we benchmark in this work. We host our MongoDB Atlas cluster on Amazon Web Service (AWS) with the region Sydney (ap-southeast-2). For cluster tier, we use Dedicated Development Clusters M10, which has 2 GB RAM, 10 GB storage, and 0.2 vCPU. The MongoDB version deployed by Atlas cluster is 3.6 with WiredTiger. The replication factor is 3, which means that all data in our MongoDB Atlas instance are replicated three times and put on different nodes.

The Amazon Web Service (AWS) Elastic Compute Cloud (EC2)[2] is used to run our benchmark application. The instance we choose is c4.2xlarge with Ubuntu Server 16.04 LTS (HVM) as the operation system. c4.2xlarge contains 32 GB RAM, 8 GB storage, 8 vCPUs, and the network performance is "high". The EC2 instance is also deployed in Sydney (ap-southeast-2) to ensure to lowest network latency possible.

4 Benchmarking Results

In this section, we record the benchmarking results for the MongoDB Atlas. We have measured with three different reading preferences: *primary*, *secondary*, and *nearest*. As we mentioned in Sect. 2, the architecture of MongoDB Atlas is, all writes go to the primary copy, and then the latest value propagates to all secondary copies. We use the default write concern (1) in all experiments. The reads, however, are configured in several ways in our experiments, including *primary* (which is the default one), *secondary*, and *nearest*.

We first show the read and write operation latency, and then report the measured consistency results for three different reading preference configurations: *primary*, *secondary*, and *nearest*.

4.1 Writing and Reading Latency

In this subsection, we analyze the writing and the reading latency. As we use three different read preference configurations: *primary*, *secondary*, and *nearest*, we are very interested in the actual read latency of those three settings.

Figure 4 shows the cumulative distribution function (CDF) of read and write operation latency. From this graph, we can see that a large proportion of reading requests finish within in the first few milliseconds. But there is not much difference for the latency among three reading preferences. We have also calculated the average read and write operation latency in Table 1. From that table, we can also reach the same conclusion.

The reason for lack of a latency advantage of reading from the nearest copy might be that both our benchmarking machine and the MongoDB Atlas instance

---

[2] https://aws.amazon.com/ec2/.

are in the same region. Moreover, the MongoDB Atlas instance is not geographically distributed.

The cumulative distribution function (CDF) of write operation latency is
also recorded in Fig. 4 and the average write operation latency is displayed in
Table 1 as well. Note that in our three experiments, the writing configurations
are always the same.

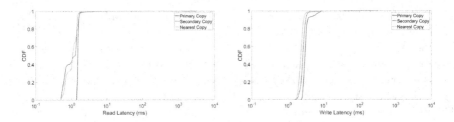

Fig. 4. Read and write operation latency

Table 1. Average read and write operation latency (ms)

	Read at primary copy	Read at secondary copy	Read at nearest copy
Read latency	1.61	1.15	1.15
Write latency	3.30	2.75	2.42

4.2   Reading from the Primary Copy

In the first study, we deploy the writer and the reader in the same EC2 instance,
but in different processes. Both the AWS EC2 instance and the MongoDB Atlas
cluster are deployed in Sydney (ap-southeast-2). In fact, we are not sure whether
the MongoDB Atlas cluster and AWS EC2 instance are in the same data center
or not, but putting them in the same geographic region should help reduce the
impact of the network latency.

In this experiment, all writes and reads go to the primary copy of MongoDB
Atlas, which are the default settings.

We run our benchmarking application for 550 "measurements", which contains around 27,500,000 reads and 15,950 writes. The total running time is more
than 30 h.

Our analysis shows that no inconsistent reads are observed, when all the
writing and reading requests are sent to the primary copy of MongoDB Atlas.

4.3   Reading from the Secondary Copy

In the second study, we again put a writer and a reader in the same EC2 instance,
yet in different processes. This time all writing requests are sent to the primary

copy of MongoDB as usual, however, the reading requests are sent to the secondary copies only.

We run our benchmarking application for 2,200 "measurements" in this circumstance, which contains around 110,000,000 reads and 63,800 writes. The total benchmarking time is around 120 h.

When all reading requests are sent to the secondary copies, we are able to observe some inconsistent reads.

The blue dash line in Fig. 5 shows the probability of reading a stale value from the secondary copies. The scale of Y axis is logarithmic. Although the time window between two writes are 3,000 ms, in Fig. 5, we only display the curve for the first 27 ms. This is because after 27 ms each data point is only backed up by a few stale reads (1 or 2 stale reads). The inconsistency probability is then unreliable. If we would like to see a nice curve, we would have to run the benchmarking application for around 10 times longer, so that one or two inconsistent reads by chance does not have a huge impact on the results.

From the blue dash line in Fig. 5, we are able see that the probability of reading stale value starts at a very high number, which is more than 0.9 within the first millisecond. The probability drops rapidly between 3 ms and 5 ms - from 0.795 to 0.019. After that, the number goes down gradually.

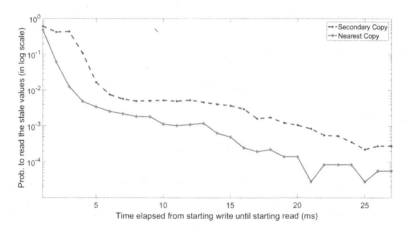

Fig. 5. Probability of reading stale value from secondary and nearest copy (Color figure online)

There is also one interesting observation. We refer to one write and all subsequent reads as one "period". There are two horrendous "periods" observed during our experiments (shown in Fig. 6). Figure 6(A) shows the first horrendous "period". The vertical axis displays the number of subsequent reads. The first horrendous "period" lasts for around 526 ms. In the first 481 ms, the values returned are two versions old (shown in green) and there are 385 reads in total. In the next 45 ms, the values got back are one version old (shown in light green), and there are 36 reads here. The second horrendous "period" is around 241 ms long, with 160 inconsistent reads in it, and all of them are one version old. For both of these two "periods", the number of stale reads is extremely large compared to other normal "periods", which usually only contains around three to five stale reads.

One possibility for the cause of the horrendous periods, is if replicas fail to receive an oplog entry; if so, reads would see older versions until the oplog-containing message was successfully retransmitted. It has been suggested that 240 ms is approximately the timing till retransmission in the TCP protocol in the Atlas setting as it was configured. If so, the horrendous period lasting 481 ms would represent the first retransmission also being lost. Further investigation is desirable for these cases.

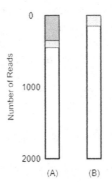

Fig. 6. Two horrendous "periods" (Color figure online)

4.4   Reading from the Nearest Copy

In this experiment, we benchmark the data consistency when the *read preference* is set to *nearest*. Again, we put a writer and a reader in the same AWS EC2 instance, but in different processes. MongoDB Atlas should be able to find the copy which is closest to the driver and return a value to it as soon as possible.

Similar to our second experiment, we have 2,200 "measurements" in this circumstance, and it contains about 110,000,000 reads and 63,800 writes. The total benchmarking time is more than 120 h.

The red concrete line in Fig. 5 displays the probability of read stale value from the nearest copy. Similar to the probability of reading stale value from the secondary copies, the probability of reading inconsistent data starts quite high at beginning, which is more than 0.9 within the first milliseconds. It goes down fairly quick to 0.017 at 3 ms, and then drops gradually. The value becomes stable after 20 ms, which is around 10^{-5}.

Comparing the probability of read stale value within two situations, we can see that the probability of reading stale value from nearest copy is slightly lower than the probability from the secondary copies.

5   Discussion

In this section, we provide a short discussion on the decisions we made for doing the data analysis phase, and why our method is slightly different that that used in prior work on other stores [19].

5.1   Dealing with the Extreme Low Inconsistency Rates

As you can see in Sect. 4, starting at a short period after a write, there is a very low probability of reading stale values from either secondary copies or the nearest copy. The number is around 10^{-3} to 10^{-4}. So it will be rare for an application to observe an inconsistent read (this is good for developers), but for us it becomes challenging to a get a stable calculation of such a low inconsistency probability - sometimes you can have one extra or fewer stale read just by chance, which can make the data points in a graph fluctuate a lot when each represents only a few such reads.

Our solution to this problem is to run the benchmarking application for a long time, to make sure that each data points in Fig. 5 is backed up by enough (say more than 10) stale reads. In this case, one more or less stale reads tends not to have a huge impact on our probability calculations.

5.2   Excluding "Overlapping" Reads and Writes

As mentioned, we eliminate all cases of "overlapping" between a write and subsequent read operations - we only report that a read gets a stale value, if at the time the reading request is sent out, the writing request before it has already returned (shown in Fig. 7(B)). Figure 7(A) demonstrates the excluded cases, with "overlapping" writing and reading requests. In the situation of the blue solid line, the reading request reaches MongoDB Atlas after the writing request reached the distributed system. If we observe a stale value in a case like this, it would represent an inconsistency. However, for the case of the blue dash line, although the reading request is sent out later than the writing request, it "hits" the distributed system earlier than the writing request. In this case, we would not see the write for sure, and so return of the previous value isn't evidence of inconsistency among the replicas.

But the fact is, we cannot tell from observations at the consumer side, whether a stale value we get in Fig. 7(A) belongs to the case of the solid line or the situation of the dash line. So we eliminate all "overlapping" reading and writing requests from inclusion as stale reads.

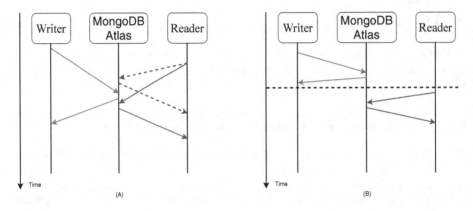

Fig. 7. Message diagram for overlapping writing and reading requests (Color figure online)

6 Related Work

Due to the limitation of the CAP theorem or the PACELC formulation [4,12], people usually sacrifice data consistency for availability or low latency in distributed storage systems. On the other hand, understand the data consistency behavior is of vital importance for the developers. As a result, there are many works focusing on benchmark the consistency performance of various distributed storage systems. In general, there are three categories of consistency benchmark: empirical measurement, trace analysis, and prediction [14,15].

Wada et al. [19] propose to benchmark distributed storage systems from the customers' view. They set a writer updating the current time stamp into an item, and the frequency is once every three seconds. The reader reads 50 times each second. Each "measurement" runs for 5 min. They repeat their experiments once every hour for a week. They benchmark a number of distributed storage systems, including Amazon SimpleDB[3], Amazon S3[4], Azure Table[5] and Blob Storage[6], and Google App Engine Datastore[7]. They have observed very interesting consistency behaviour in Amazon SimpleDB, however, there were no inconsistent reads recorded in other distributed data storages. Our work use a similar method as Wada's with a few differences described above.

Bermbach et al. [8,9,11] use a slightly different approach. Instead of updating the value in the item for a specific time period, Bermbach et al. do not update the value until "the old value no longer returns". They set the maximum time interval between two successive writes as 100 s. They benchmark Amazon S3,

---

[3] https://aws.amazon.com/simpledb/.

[4] https://aws.amazon.com/s3.

[5] https://azure.microsoft.com/en-au/services/storage/tables/.

[6] https://azure.microsoft.com/en-au/services/storage/blobs/.

[7] https://cloud.google.com/appengine/.

and got some interesting results. After the original experiment, they contacted Amazon, who quickly changed their service behavior [10].

Polygraph [5] is a framework which allows empirical benchmarking of transactional consistency. Rather than defining a particular workload (as in [8,19], or the current paper), Polygraph is combined with a workload from an existing benchmark. The workload is typically one that was originally aimed at performance, such as TPC-C or YCSB; during execution, Polygraph captures the trace of operations on various entities (chosen by the user), and then post-execution analysis determines whether an equivalent serial execution would give the same result in each read; if not an anomaly is reported.

Trace analysis is another method to observe inconsistency. It observes the trace of a workload, and then checks whether it meets the definition [14]. Trace analysis can be used to measure the actual impact of inconsistency and the amount of inconsistency varies when the workload changes. Golab et al. [16] propose a trace analysis method and a novel consistency metric called Γ consistency. According to the authors, Γ consistency can be used to detect how often consistency anomalies occur and how bad they are. Lu et al. [17] conduct trace analysis on the real data from Facebook. They first log operations on a subset of some items, and then check trace for a few consistency guarantees, including linearizable, read-my-write, etc.

In addition to empirical measurement and trace analysis, there are a few researchers going a step further. They model and predict the consistency performance. Usually, they first design a model, and then use Monte Carlo simulation to predict the performance. Bailis et al. [6,7] propose the Probabilistically Bounded Staleness (PBS) model to simulate consistency behavior on Dynamo-style [13] quorum system. They present a model called WARS, and implement the simulation using Monte Carlo Simulation. The PBS model can be used to predict the probability of seeing stale value against the network and in-system latency. However, the Probabilistically Bounded Staleness (PBS) model does not consider the operation failures. Bermbach [8] proposes a more general prediction model, which can predict more than Dynamo-style quorum system and can somewhat handle operation failures.

7   Conclusion

In this paper, we benchmark the data consistency properties of MongoDB Atlas which is a Document Storage as a Service (DSaaS). The benchmarking results show that (as expected) there are no inconsistent reads if the data is accessed from the primary copy, but some inconsistent reads are observed if the data is retrieved from the secondary copies and the nearest copy. The probability of reading a stale value decreases briskly with duration since the latest write, as replicas are caught up to the primary. Within a few milliseconds, the probability of a stale read is only a few percent. We also observed one or two writes where propagation somehow failed, and so subsequent reads continued to see stale values for a very long time.

We also look at the operation latency, and we find there is no significant improvement in read latency when reading from the nearest copy, in the cases where the benchmarking application and the MongoDB Atlas cluster are in the same region. On the other hand, the consistency performance of reading from the nearest copy is worse than reading from the primary copy. So we may conclude that sacrificing consistency for low latency is not sensible, if the application and the MongoDB Atlas cluster are in the same region and the cluster is not geographically distributed.

Acknowledgments. This research forms part of the Australian Research Council (ARC) Linkage Project LP160100883. We thank Gary Little, Shahram Ghandeharizadeh, and Raghunath Nambiar for their comments on this paper. We also thank AWS Cloud Research Credits for their support.

References

1. Read preference - mongodb manual. https://docs.mongodb.com/manual/core/read-preference/. Accessed 02 June 2018
2. Write concern - mongodb manual. https://docs.mongodb.com/manual/reference/write-concern/. Accessed 02 June 2018
3. Write concern for replica sets - mongodb manual. https://docs.mongodb.com/manual/core/replica-set-write-concern/. Accessed 02 June 2018
4. Abadi, D.: Consistency tradeoffs in modern distributed database system design: cap is only part of the story. Computer **45**(2), 37–42 (2012)
5. Alabdulkarim, Y., Almaymoni, M., Ghandeharizadeh, S.: Polygraph. Technical report 2017-02, Database Laboratory, Computer Science Department, University of Southern California (2017)
6. Bailis, P., Venkataraman, S., Franklin, M.J., Hellerstein, J.M., Stoica, I.: Probabilistically bounded staleness for practical partial quorums. Proc. VLDB Endow. **5**(8), 776–787 (2012)
7. Bailis, P., Venkataraman, S., Franklin, M.J., Hellerstein, J.M., Stoica, I.: Quantifying eventual consistency with PBS. VLDB J. **23**(2), 279–302 (2014)
8. Bermbach, D.: Benchmarking eventually consistent distributed storage systems (2014)
9. Bermbach, D., Tai, S.: Eventual consistency: how soon is eventual? An evaluation of Amazon S3's consistency behavior. In: Proceedings of the 6th Workshop on Middleware for Service Oriented Computing, p. 1. ACM (2011)
10. Bermbach, D., Tai, S.: Benchmarking eventual consistency: lessons learned from long-term experimental studies. In: 2014 IEEE International Conference on Cloud Engineering (IC2E), pp. 47–56. IEEE (2014)
11. Bermbach, D., Wittern, E., Tai, S.: Cloud Service Benchmarking. Springer, Heidelberg (2017). https://doi.org/10.1007/978-3-319-55483-9
12. Brewer, E.A.: Towards robust distributed systems. In: PODC, vol. 7 (2000)
13. DeCandia, G., et al.: Dynamo: Amazon's highly available key-value store. In: ACM SIGOPS Operating Systems Review, vol. 41, pp. 205–220. ACM (2007)
14. Fekete, A.: Consumer-view of consistency properties: definition, measurement, and exploitation. https://www2.ucsc.edu/papoc-2016/Fekete-PaPoC-London.pdf. Accessed 03 June 2018

15. Golab, W., Rahman, M.R., AuYoung, A., Keeton, K., Li, X.S.: Eventually consistent: not what you were expecting? Queue **12**(1), 30 (2014)
16. Golab, W., Rahman, M.R., AuYoung, A., Keeton, K., Gupta, I.: Client-centric benchmarking of eventual consistency for cloud storage systems. In: 2014 IEEE 34th International Conference on Distributed Computing Systems (ICDCS), pp. 493–502. IEEE (2014)
17. Lu, H., et al.: Existential consistency: measuring and understanding consistency at Facebook. In: Proceedings of the 25th Symposium on Operating Systems Principles, pp. 295–310. ACM (2015)
18. Shukla, D., et al.: Schema-agnostic indexing with Azure DocumentDB. Proc. VLDB Endow. **8**(12), 1668–1679 (2015)
19. Wada, H., Fekete, A., Zhao, L., Lee, K., Liu, A.: Data consistency properties and the trade-offs in commercial cloud storage: the consumers' perspective. In: CIDR, vol. 11, pp. 134–143 (2011)

Lessons Learned from the Industry's First TPC Benchmark DS (TPC-DS)

Manan Trivedi[1(✉)] and Zhenqiang Chen[2(✉)]

[1] Cisco Systems, Inc., 275 East Tasman Drive, San Jose, CA 95134, USA
matrived@cisco.com
[2] Transwarp Technology (Shanghai) Co., Ltd.,
11F&12F, Bld B, No. 88 Hongcao RD, Shanghai, China
zhenqiang.chen@transwarp.io

Abstract. The TPC Benchmark DS (TPC-DS) is a decision support benchmark that models several generally applicable aspects of a decision support system, including queries and data maintenance, which is representative of modern decision support and big data applications. TPC-DS was initially designed for Relational Database Management Systems (RDBMS), later extended support for Apache Hadoop. This paper provides the lessons learned including hardware and software tuning parameters from the first TPC-DS publication which was on Cisco UCS® Integrated Infrastructure with Transwarp Data Hub.

Keywords: Industry standards · Performance · Hadoop · Data warehouse
TPC-DS

1 Introduction

The TPC Benchmark DS (TPC-DS) is a decision support benchmark that models several generally applicable aspects of a decision support system [1]. "It is intended to provide a fair and honest comparison of various vendor implementations by providing highly comparable, controlled and repeatable tasks in evaluating the performance of decision support systems (DSS). Its workload is expected to test the upward boundaries of hardware system performance in the areas of CPU utilization, memory utilization, I/O subsystem utilization and the ability of the operating system and database software to perform various complex functions important to DSS - examine large volumes of data, compute and execute the best execution plan for queries with a high degree of complexity" [2]. From Version 2, TPC-DS benchmark was extended for big data system.

Hundreds of publications have been written by academia and industry on various aspects of the workloads leading to innovation, better performance and lower price per performance systems. Also, some vendors have published, only in blogs, cherry-picking performance measures of a small subset of the full TPC-DS benchmark, or with many modifications to the queries. There has been no fully audited TPC-DS benchmark published until "Cisco UCS Publishes the First Ever Audited Result of the TPC-DS Benchmark with Transwarp Hadoop" [4]. The benchmark was run on Cisco UCS Integrated Infrastructure for Big Data and Analytics, and Transwarp Data Hub v5.1. It

© Springer Nature Switzerland AG 2019
R. Nambiar and M. Poess (Eds.): TPCTC 2018, LNCS 11135, pp. 140–154, 2019.
https://doi.org/10.1007/978-3-030-11404-6_11

achieves, at a 10,000 GB scale factor, a composite query per hour of 1,580,649 QphDS and a price/performance of $0.64 USD/QphDS [5]. See Table 1.

Table 1. TPC-DS with Cisco UCS and transwarp data hub

Date Submitted	Scale Factor	Company	System	qphds	Price/qphds	Watts/Kqphds	System Availability	Database	Operating System	Cluster
03/05/18	10000 GB	ıl|ıı|lı CISCO	Cisco UCS Integrated Infrastructure for Big Data	1,580,649	.64 USD	NR	03/05/18	Transwarp Data Hub v5.1	Red Hat Enterprise Linux Server 6.7	Y

2 Transwarp Data Hub

Apache Hadoop started as a framework to store and process very large data sets in a distributed manner in a cost-effective way. Initially, this distributed data processing was limited to batch processing only. More recently, tools have been developed that extend the power of Hadoop big data processing directly into the realm of decision support systems or for a Data Warehouse. In recent years, the explosion of data has strained traditional decision support systems with enterprises looking beyond traditional data warehouse for their needs. Compared with traditional data warehouse, modern data warehouse have several advantages, such as scalability, processing semi/non-structure data, real-time processing, analysis and judgment, Data mining and deep learning.

The Transwarp Data Hub (TDH) is a full suite of Hadoop distribution components, including a supplemental SQL engine (Inceptor), machine learning & deep learning components, a NoSQL search engine and stream processing. Figure 1 shows a logical data view managed by Transwarp Inceptor in logic data warehouse (LDW). In this framework, Transwarp Inceptor unifies the SQL interfaces. It analyzes all data from different sources through SQL with dialects support for different RDMS. It also extends the SQL for full text search and streaming from remote Kafka. Inceptor SQL engine supports both standard SQL and stored procedures (like Oracle PL/SQL). After semantics analysis, the Inceptor optimizer will optimize the SQLs with CBO, RBO etc. The optimized execution plan will be sent to Inceptor vectorized and distribution execution engine. In the data access layer, Inceptor provides drivers to access different kind of databases and data on HDFS. All the data are in a unified view managed by Metadata management.

In modern DW, SQL is still the most popular ETL approach and query. TPC-DS is still the most popular benchmark for most big data vendors.

3 TPC-DS

TPC-DS benchmark workloads include 99 queries; but the benchmark test is not just about those queries. The test process and metrics include the following six steps (refer TPC-DS Specification for more detail [3]):

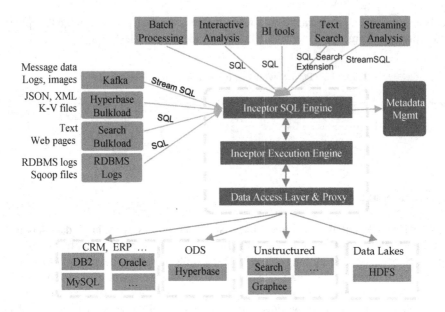

Fig. 1. Logical data view managed by Transwarp Inceptor in LDW

- Data Load test (LD).
- Power test (PT), which runs the 99 queries in one stream.
- Throughput test 1 (TT1), which runs the 99 queries in multiple streams.
- Maintenance test 1 (DM1), which updates the databases with the refresh functions.
- Throughput test 2 (TT2), which reruns the 99 queries in multiple streams.
- Maintenance test (DM2), which re-updates the databases with the refresh functions.

The 99 queries are defined as templates. Each query has several parameters which are determined by dsqgen with SEED, specifically "is selected as the timestamp of the end of the database load time (Load End Time) expressed in the format mmddhh-mmsss". This timestamp "guarantees that the query substitution parameter values are not known prior to running". In addition to the parameters, the query orders of different streams are different. Figure 2 shows the execution order

Fig. 2. TPC-DS execution order

Let

- SF be the scale factor in the benchmark test, which might be 1000, 3000, 10000, etc.
- S_q be the number of streams executed in a Throughput test.
- T_{Load} be the data load time.
- T_{Power} be the Power test time.
- T_{TT1} be the first Throughput test time.
- T_{TT2} be the second Throughput test time.
- T_{DM1} be the first Maintenance test time.
- T_{DM2} be the second Maintenance test time.
- $Q = S_q * 99$

The primary performance metric of the benchmark is QphDS@SF, the effective sort throughput of the benchmarked configuration. Here is an example (using the summation method):

$$QphDS@SF = \left\lfloor \frac{SF * Q}{\sqrt[4]{T_{PT} * T_{TT} * T_{DM} * T_{LD}}} \right\rfloor$$

Here,

- $T_{TT} = T_{TT1} + T_{TT2}$
- $T_{DM} = T_{DM1} + T_{DM2}$
- $T_{PT} = T_{Power} * S_q$
- $T_{LD} = 0.01 * S_q * T_{Load}$
- T_{PT}, T_{TT}, T_{DM} and T_{LD} quantities are in units of decimal hours with a resolution of at least a second.

The price-to-performance metric for the benchmark is defined as follows:

$$\$/QphDS@SF = \frac{P}{QphDS@SF}$$

Here, P is the total cost of ownership (TCO) of the system under test (SUT). TPC-DS also reports the following numerical quantities:

- Execution time of each query in each stream.
- Execution time of each refresh function in maintenance tests.

4   System Under Test (SUT)

The tests were conducted a series of TPC-DS to characterize the performance in various deployment scenarios. The test configuration consisted of Cisco UCS Integrated Infrastructure for Big Data and Analytics cluster with 17 Cisco UCS C240 M4 Rack Servers. The Cisco UCS Integrated Infrastructure for Big Data and Analytics is built using the following components:

- Cisco UCS 6296UP 96-Port Fabric Interconnect: Fabric interconnects are central to the Cisco Unified Computing System™ (Cisco UCS). They provide low-latency, lossless 10 Gigabit Ethernet, Fibre Channel over Ethernet (FCoE), and Fibre Channel functions with management capabilities for the system. All servers attached to fabric interconnects become part of a single, highly available management domain.
- Cisco UCS C240 M4 Rack Server: Cisco UCS C-Series Rack Servers extend Cisco UCS in standard rack-mount form factors. The Cisco UCS C240 M4 Rack Server is designed to support a wide range of computing, I/O, and storage-capacity demands in a compact design. It supports two Intel® Xeon® processor E5-2600 v4 series CPUs, up to 1.5 TB of memory, and 24 small-form-factor (SFF) disk drives plus two internal SATA boot drives and Cisco UCS Virtual Interface Card (VIC) 1387 adapters.

The System under test configuration consists of two Cisco UCS 6296 fabric interconnects, 17 Cisco UCS C240 M4 servers with two Intel Xeon processor E5-2680 v4 series CPUs, 512 GB of memory, and 24 SFF disk drives plus two internal SATA boot drives and Cisco UCS VIC 1287 adapters, as shown in Fig. 3. Table 2 lists the software versions used.

Table 2. Software versions

Layer	Component	Version or release
Software	Red Hat Enterprise Linux (RHEL) server	Version 6.7 (x86_64)
	Cisco UCS manager	Release 3.1(1 g)
DBMS	Transwarp data hub	Version 5.1

5 Test Results

The details of the test results are shown in Table 3.

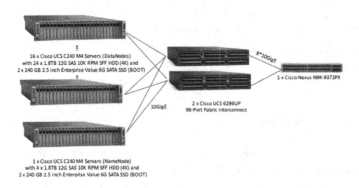

Fig. 3. SUT cluster configuration

6   Hardware and Software: Performance Characterization

In the following section, we will do an in-depth performance analysis with various permutations of these hardware and software. Many factors come into play when tuning a system as complex as big data systems. Performance tuning involves making modifications to hardware, software, and network.

Infrastructure tuning helps achieve optimal utilization of resources. It also helps the application run faster and perform better.

- Server
  - BIOS
    - CPU parameters
    - Intel Turbo Boost Technology
    - Intel Hyper-Threading Technology
    - Prefetcher
    - C-states
    - Power control policy
    - Memory tuning
- Network
  - Network tuning parameters
  - Network interface card (NIC) bonding
  - Jumbo frame (maximum transmission unit [MTU])
- Storage
  - RAID 0
    - Write back
    - Read ahead
    - Stripe size
  - JBOD
  - JBOD Versus RAID 0

6.1   Operating System

OS performance tuning is used to manage and improve resources that respond to individual requests. OS scalability is managed by monitoring the resource consumption of varying volumes of requests, from low to very high, by changing default OS settings.

- File system
  - XFS
  - Agcount
  - Mount
  - Fstab
- Post-OS tuning
  - sysctl.conf
  - limits.conf
  - CPU frequency and scaling governor
  - Transparent huge pages
  - Linux swappiness
  - I/O scheduler

Table 3. TPC-DS test results

Name	Value	Unit
Scale Factor (SF)	10,000	GB
Streams	4	Stream
Queries (Q)	396	Queries
T_load	4,778.8	Second
T_ld	0.0531	Hour
T_pt	24.0173	Hour
T_tt1	66,440.1	Second
T_tt2	68,173.3	Second
T_dm1	1,502.9	Second
T_dm2	1,471.0	Second
T_tt	37.3927	Hour
T_dm	0.8261	Hour

Load Step	Start	End	(sec.)	(hh:mm:ss)
Build	01/23/18 19:22:46.21	01/23/18 20:38:19.77	4,533.56	1:15:34
Audit	01/23/18 20:38:19.77	01/23/18 22:12:48.93	5,669.16	1:34:29
Get Stats	01/23/18 22:12:48.93	01/23/18 22:16:54.15	245.22	0:04:05
Reported	01/23/18 19:22:46.21	01/23/18 22:16:54.15	4,778.78	1:19:39

Test	Start	End	(sec.)	(hh:mm:ss)
Power	01/23/18 22:28:21.92	01/24/18 04:28:37.41	21,615.49	6:00:15
Thruput-1	01/24/18 04:28:37.41	01/24/18 22:55:57.42	66,440.01	18:27:20
Thruput-2	01/24/18 23:21:00.31	01/25/18 18:17:13.57	68,173.26	18:56:13
DM-1	01/24/18 22:55:57.42	01/24/18 23:21:00.30	1,502.88	0:25:03
DM-2	01/25/18 18:17:13.57	01/25/18 18:41:44.52	1,470.95	0:24:31

Stream	Start	End	(sec.)	(hh:mm:ss)
Pt - 0	01/23/18 22:28:21.92	01/24/18 04:28:37.41	21,615.49	6:00:15
Tt1 - 1	01/24/18 04:28:37.41	01/24/18 22:43:57.06	65,719.65	18:15:20
Tt1 - 2	01/24/18 04:28:37.42	01/24/18 22:55:57.42	66,440.00	18:27:20
Tt1 - 3	01/24/18 04:28:37.42	01/24/18 22:35:12.92	65,195.50	18:06:35
Tt1 - 4	01/24/18 04:28:37.41	01/24/18 22:34:14.87	65,137.46	18:05:37
Tt2 - 5	01/24/18 23:21:00.31	01/25/18 18:09:14.08	67,693.77	18:48:14
Tt2 - 6	01/24/18 23:21:00.31	01/25/18 18:15:04.29	68,043.98	18:54:04
Tt2 - 7	01/24/18 23:21:00.31	01/25/18 18:13:57.73	67,977.42	18:52:57
Tt2 - 8	01/24/18 23:21:00.31	01/25/18 18:17:13.57	68,173.26	18:56:13
DMt1 - 1	01/24/18 22:55:57.42	01/24/18 23:09:58.30	840.88	0:14:01
DMt1 - 2	01/24/18 23:09:58.30	01/24/18 23:21:00.30	662.00	0:11:02
DMt2 - 3	01/25/18 18:17:13.57	01/25/18 18:29:41.85	748.28	0:12:28
DMt2 - 4	01/25/18 18:29:41.85	01/25/18 18:41:44.52	722.67	0:12:03

6.2   Server Tuning

Hadoop is based on a new approach to storing and processing complex data, with data movement reduced. Hadoop distributes the data across the cluster that each machine in a Hadoop cluster stores, and it also processes the data. Therefore, it is important to tune the processing, or computing, aspect of the system to achieve optimal performance from the cluster.

BIOS settings can have a significant performance impact, depending on the workload and the applications. Table 4 lists the optimal CPU settings for Hadoop based on the tests reported in this document.

Table 4. Optimal CPU settings

Parameter	Setting
Intel turbo boost	Enabled
Enhanced intel speedstep	Enabled
Intel hyper-threading	Enabled
Core multiprocessing	All
Virtualization technology	Disabled
Hardware prefetcher	Enabled
Adjacent cache line prefetcher	Enabled
Data Cache Unit (DCU) streamer prefetcher	Enabled
DCU IP prefetcher	Enabled
Direct cache access	Enabled
Processor C-State	Disabled
CPU performance	Enterprise
Power technology	Performance
Energy performance	Performance
Frequency floor override	Enabled
P-state coordination	Hw-all
DRAM clock throttling	Performance

Table 5 lists optimal memory settings for Hadoop based on the tests reported here.

Table 5. Optimal Memory Settings

Parameter	Setting
Memory RAS configuration	Maximum performance
NUMA	Enabled
Low-voltage double data rate (LV DDR) mode	Performance mode
DRAM refresh rate	1 time
DDR3 voltage selection	Platform default

6.3   Network Tuning

The impact of the network on big data is enormous. An efficient and resilient network is a crucial part of a good Hadoop cluster because the network is what connects all the nodes. The network is also crucial for writing data, reading data, and signaling and for HDFS operations A job may need to be restarted, or a workload may be pushed to the remaining nodes, resulting in delay. Therefore, networks must be designed to provide redundancy, with multiple paths between computing nodes, and they must be able to scale.

Table 6 lists some network performance settings that can increase Hadoop performance. These options increase the read and write cache sizes for the network stack. These parameters can be tested with the **systctl –w** command or made permanent by adding the variable to the /etc./sysctl.conf file.

Table 6. Optimal network tuning parameters for hadoop

Parameter	Tuned value	Description
net.core.somaxconn	1024	Changing the net.core.somaxconn Linux kernel settings from the default of 128 to 1024 helps with burst requests from the name node and job tracker. This option sets the size of the listening queue, or the number of connections that the server can set up at one time
net.ipv4.tcp_retries2	5	This variable helps forward the packets between interfaces. This variable is special; its change resets all configuration parameters to their default state
net.core.rmem_max	16777216	These settings increase the TCP maximum buffer size. The four options shown here increase the TCP send and receive buffers, allowing an application to move its data out faster so it can serve other requests. This adjustment also improves the client's ability to send data to the server when it gets busy
net.core.wmem_max	16777216	
net.ipv4.tcp_rmem	16777216	
net.ipv4.tcp_wmem	16777216	
net.core. netdev_max_backlog	10000	The netdev_max_backlog is a queue within the Linux kernel where traffic is stored after reception from the NIC, but before processing by the protocol stacks (IP, TCP) etc.

You can tune NIC bonding. A NIC is a computer hardware component that connects a computer to a computer network. Network bonding is a method of combining (joining) two or more network interfaces together into a single interface. This combination increases network throughput and provides redundancy. If one interface is down or unplugged, the remaining interfaces will keep the network traffic up and alive. Network bonding can be used in situations in which you need redundancy, fault tolerance, or load balancing.

Linux allows bonding of multiple network interfaces into a single channel using a special kernel module called a bonding module. The Linux bonding driver provides a method for aggregating multiple network interfaces into a single logical "bonded" interface. The behavior of the bonded interface depends on the mode. In general, the mode provides either hot-standby or load-balancing services. Additionally, link-integrity monitoring can be performed.

7   Transwarp Inceptor Tuning Parameters

The key production used in the test is Transwarp Inceptor. The database is in ORC format, which is stored on HDFS. Figure 4 show the architecture of Inceptor.

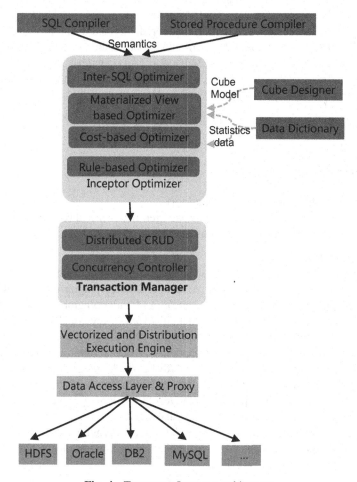

Fig. 4. Transwarp Inceptor architecture

7.1 HDFS Tuning

During Maintenance test 1, the auditor will select a disk to make it no accessible. To make the HDFS work without reporting error, the parameter dfs.datanode.failed.volumes.tolerated must be set a value greater or equal than 1.

Note: By default, HDFS data replication is 3. One disk fail does not impact the data access.

For better IO throughput, the HDFS Data node should use all the data disks. dfs.datanode.data.dir is set as:

/data/disk1/hadoop/data, /data/disk10/hadoop/data, /data/disk11/hadoop/data, /data/disk12/hadoop/data, /data/disk13/hadoop/data, /data/disk14/hadoop/data, /data/disk15/hadoop/data, /data/disk16/hadoop/data, /data/disk17/hadoop/data, /data/disk18/hadoop/data, /data/disk19/hadoop/data, /data/disk2/hadoop/data, /data/disk20/hadoop/data, /data/disk21/hadoop/data, data/disk22/hadoop/data, /data/disk23/hadoop/data, /data/disk24/hadoop/data, /data/disk3/hadoop/data, /data/disk4/hadoop/data, /data/disk5/hadoop/data, /data/disk6/hadoop/data, /data/disk7/hadoop/data, /data/disk8/hadoop/data, /data/disk9/hadoop/data

All other HDFS parameters do not have big impact for the test and ban be set as default values.

7.2 Transwarp Inceptor Tuning

(1) Inceptor shuffle directories configuration
Similar as the Data node configuration, to get better IO throughput, the shuffle directories are configured to use all the data disks:

EXPORT NGMR_LOCALDIR = "
/data/disk1/hadoop/ngmr/inceptorsql1, /data/disk10/hadoop/ngmr/inceptorsql1, /data/disk11/hadoop/ngmr/inceptorsql1, /data/disk12/hadoop/ngmr/inceptorsql1, /data/disk13/hadoop/ngmr/inceptorsql1, /data/disk14/hadoop/ngmr/inceptorsql1, /data/disk15/hadoop/ngmr/inceptorsql1, /data/disk16/hadoop/ngmr/inceptorsql1, /data/disk17/hadoop/ngmr/inceptorsql1, /data/disk18/hadoop/ngmr/inceptorsql1, /data/disk19/hadoop/ngmr/inceptorsql1, /data/disk2/hadoop/ngmr/inceptorsql1, /data/disk20/hadoop/ngmr/inceptorsql1, /data/disk21/hadoop/ngmr/inceptorsql1, /data/disk22/hadoop/ngmr/inceptorsql1, /data/disk23/hadoop/ngmr/inceptorsql1, /data/disk24/hadoop/ngmr/inceptorsql1, /data/disk3/hadoop/ngmr/inceptorsql1, /data/disk4/hadoop/ngmr/inceptorsql1, /data/disk5/hadoop/ngmr/inceptorsql1, /data/disk6/hadoop/ngmr/inceptorsql1, /data/disk7/hadoop/ngmr/inceptorsql1, /data/disk8/hadoop/ngmr/inceptorsql1, /data/disk9/hadoop/ngmr/inceptorsql1"

(2) Executor configuration

Tests show JVM does not work well with too many cores in one executor. And GC overhead is unacceptable if the executor is configured too much memory. In the test, 4 executors are configured for each work node, each executor is configured with 12 vcores and 32 G memory:

export INCEPTOR_YARN_EXECUTOR_MEMORY = 32000 M
export INCEPTOR_YARN_EXECUTOR_CORES = 12
export INCEPTOR_YARN_NUMBER_EXECUTORS = 64

8 Transwarp Query Optimization Tuning

In the following section, we will show how the Inceptor components apply to the TPC-DS test and do an in-depth performance analysis with Transwarp Inceptor.

8.1 SQL and Stored Procedure Compiler

Stored Procedure compiler is compatible with Oracle's PL/SQL. Users can write more complex application with procedures. The SQL compiler is compatible with SQL 2003. The 99 query templates are primarily phrased in compliance with SQL 1999 core (with OLAP amendments) [3]. So Inceptor only has 5 minor changes to run the TPC-DS workloads. Here is a summary.

- Add and use column alias: Q32 and Q92
- Add Parentheses around union all: Q2
- Ordinal position in ORDER BY replaced by column name: Q47 and Q57
- Query results are inserted in a file (clause 4.2.5): Q64

Note: These settings or changes were audited by TPC auditor and also under TPC committee

---

8.2 Optimization Tuning

Inceptor Optimizer implements lots of optimizations such as Rule Based Optimization (RBO), Cost Based Optimization (CBO), Inter-SQL-Optimization (ISO), Materialized View Based Optimization, Partition Prune and so on.

According to TPC-DS Specification [3], Materialized View Based Optimization is restricted and can only be applied to catalog_sales. And there are too combination of parameters. If taking the time to prepare view into according, Materialized view is too expensive to use in TPC-DS test. Among all the optimizations, CBO join reorder, Common Expression Elimination (CSE) and Predicate Pushdown (PPD) are the key optimizations. Without them, it is hard to PASS the 99 workload tests.

(1) Common Expression Elimination

In most cases, inner join is faster than cross join + filter. To transfer a cross join to inner join, the optimizer must identify the join conditions. This is straightforward for most workloads except query 13 and 48, in which the join condition is in an OR expression. The optimizer must extract them first. For query13, it must extract join condition:

$$ss\_hdemo\_sk = hd\_demo\_sk \text{ and } cd\_demo\_sk = ss\_cdemo\_sk$$

(2) Predicate Push Down (PPD)

The predicate push down (PPD) is a simple, but very useful optimization for performance. By pushing the predicate in join conditions or where clause down to data source, it significantly reduces the number of join result. PPD can be applied to most queries in TPC-DS test. Take query52 as an example. Figure 5(b) shows the query segment after PPD. With PPD, the result of dt join store_sales will include only one month's data. Without PPD, the result of dt join store_sales will includes all rows in store_sales except the NULL ss_sold_date_sk.

```
select ...
  from date_dim dt
      ,store_sales
      ,item
  where dt.d_date_sk = ss_sold_date_sk
      and ss_item_sk = item.i_item_sk
      and item.i_manager_id = 1
      and dt.d_moy=[MONTH]
      and dt.d_year=[YEAR]
  group by ...

        (a) Query52 segment
```

```
select ...
  from (select * from date_dim dt
          where dt.d_moy=[MONTH]
             and dt.d_year=[YEAR]) dt
      ,store_sales
      , (select * from item
          where item.i_manager_id = 1) item
  where d_date_sk = ss_sold_date_sk
      and ss_item_sk = i_item_sk
  group by ...

            (b) After PPD
```

Fig. 5. PPD example

(3) CBO Join Reorder

Lots of queries in the TPC-DS use snowflake schema. Figure 6 shows the join schema of query 72, which includes 3 fact tables and 8 dimension tables. For such pattern, join order is the key for performance. In most DBMS, join reorder is implemented as part of Cost Based Optimization (CBO) [6–9].

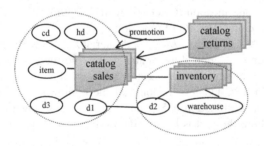

Fig. 6. Query72 join pattern

Firstly, CBO will collect statics of tables and columns by pre-analyze or dynamic samples. Then do some basic optimization and compute the cost of different join orders based on the estimation model. And finally CBO will select the join orders with the lowest cost. With CBO, the Transwarp Inceptor will join the tables in cycle (Fig. 6) first then join with other tables. Without join reorder, query 72 is out of memory (OOM).

(4) Misc Other Optimizations

In addition to the above optimizations, misc other optimizations are required to get better performance, such as window function optimization, sub-query transformation, with as optimization and vectorization.

The total tests include both single and multiply stream executions. We need some trade-off among parallel tasks to get overall better result. Here is the optimization list used in the test:

- set ngmr.o4.join = true;
- set inceptor.optimize.intersect.groupby.pushdown = true;
- set hive.window.iterator.directly = true;
- set hive.support.subquery.join.conversion.count = true;
- set inceptor.onlineiso.enabled = true;
- set ngmr.mapjoin.partitionprune = true;
- set hive.mapjoin.smalltable.filesize = 900000;
- set ngmr.partition.automerge = true;
- set hive.join.aggregateratio = 0.52;
- set mapred.minreduce.tasks = 379;
- set hive.cbo.enable = true;
- set inceptor.decimal.display.padding.zero = true;

8.3   Transaction Support

Data maintenance tests are performed as a must-have part of the benchmark execution [3]. The tests simulate the periodical synchronization with source OLTP databases [1], which is an integral part of the data warehouse lifecycle. Maintenance tests include a set of refresh runs. Refresh functions are defined in Sect. 5 of TPC-DS Specification [3], take Method 2 as an example:

> *Delete rows from * _returns with corresponding rows in * _sales*
> *where d_date between Date1 and Date2*
> *Delete rows from * _sales*
> *where d_date between Date1 and Date2*

According to the Specification [3], all the transformations must be SQL-based. As mentioned in [1], the maintenance test can be taken as the "the first industry-standard evaluation of the ETL process (Extract, Trans-formation and Load)". To support the ETL process, transaction is required for the DBMS, which is a big challenge in a distribute environment [10, 11]. Transwarp Inceptor has full transaction support, while most engines in Hadoop world do not support transaction.

9 Conclusions

TPC-DS is a challenge for any DBMS, especially for big-data tests. It is not just to run 99 queries. It covers all the stages in data warehouse. Although some optimizations are discussed in the paper, there are still lots of missing chances for better results. With more investigation, you may find more chances. In addition to the performance, the stability of the system (both hardware and software) is another challenge since the test will last long-time with high workload. This paper provides a summary of lessons learned from performance tuning for the TPC-DS benchmark. The tuning parameters have broad applicability across big data systems.

References

1. Nambiar, R., Poess, M.: The Making of TPC-DS. In: VLDB 2006 (2006)
2. Poess, M., Nambiar, R., et al.: Why you should run TPC-DS: a workload analysis. In: VLDB 2007 (2007)
3. TPC-DS specification. http://www.tpc.org/tpcds/default.asp
4. https://blogs.cisco.com/datacenter/cisco-ucs-publishes-the-first-ever-audited-result-of-the-tpc-ds-benchmark-with-hadoop
5. http://www.tpc.org/tpcds/results/tpcds_advanced_sort.asp
6. Oracle Optimizer. https://docs.oracle.com/cd/B10500_01/server.920/a96533/optimops.htm
7. Spark CBO. https://issues.apache.org/jira/browse/SPARK-16026
8. Hortonworks Hive. https://hortonworks.com/blog/hive-0-14-cost-based-optimizer-cbo-technical-overview/
9. DB2 Optimizer. https://www.ibm.com/developerworks/data/library/techarticle/dm-1025db2accessplan/index.htm
10. Fox, A., Brewer, E.: Harvest, yield and scalable tolerant systems. In: Proceedings of 7th Workshop Hot Topics in Operating Systems (HotOS 1999), pp. 174–178. IEEE CS (1999)
11. Brewer, E.: CAP twelve years later: how the "rules" have changed. Computer 45(2), 23–29 (2012)
12. http://www.transwarp.io/about/download?lang=en

Author Index

Printed in the United States
By Bookmasters